Miami Symposium on the Prediction of Behavior, 1968

Miami Symposium on the Prediction of Behavior, 1968: *Effects of Early Experience*

EDITED BY
Marshall R. Jones

UNIVERSITY OF MIAMI PRESS
Coral Gables, Florida

Contents

Preface

THE PAPERS in this volume were presented originally at a symposium held at the University of Miami in December of 1968. The symposium was supported in part by funds made available through the National Institutes of Health Biomedical Sciences Grant to the University of Miami.

The 1968 symposium was organized on a slightly different pattern than was the first one in this series. In the present instance, major papers were presented by Sackett, Denenberg, and Sigel on certain areas of research dealing with the effects of early experience on later behavior, and then prepared comments on these papers were supplied by Meier, Darby, and Smock. An additional paper was presented at the symposium by Stanley Coopersmith on the effects of early experience on later personality patterns, but Dr. Coopersmith was unable to provide a manuscript of his presentation in time for inclusion in this volume. Vernon Van De Riet of the University of Florida had agreed to comment on the Coopersmith paper, but since it was not available to him, he necessarily confined his remarks at the symposium to some general issues in this field.

Since each of the major papers in this volume is accompanied by a detailed comment from another researcher actively engaged in the field, it would be presumptious of me to undertake a detailed review of them here. It will suffice to draw to your attention the fact that there has been a remarkable increase in the amount of experimental data available on the effects of early experience on later behavior within the last few years, that this is an area of immense significance both for theory and methodology in psychology, and that each of the participants in this symposium has been in the forefront of the new developments in this field and can speak as an authority. There is considerable material reported in these papers that has not previously been published. At least as important as the new material, I suspect, are some of the new concepts and proposals that are introduced and discussed. Sackett, for example, in addition to reporting new research findings, gives one of the most thorough and most succinct statements of criteria for valid research in this field that I have seen anywhere. It undoubtedly will make much of the future research in this field more definitive. Denenberg has taken a long stride toward accomplishing what many of us for years have been insisting must be done toward integrating the "two psychologies" by using experimental techniques for creating individual differences and "programmed" life histories. And as still another example, Sigel offers some exciting new approaches to the conceptualization of how discriminations are formed and lead to representational competence. There is much stimulating reading, both in the major papers and in the comments on them.

On behalf of the Department of Psychology, I should like to express appreciation to the University of Miami NIH Biomedical Sciences Grant Committee for financial support of the symposium at which the papers included here were presented, to the administration of the University of Miami that encouraged this symposium in several ways, and to my colleagues in the department for their assistance in selecting the symposium participants and making the arrangements necessary for such a meeting.

MARSHALL R. JONES

Miami Symposium on the Prediction of Behavior, 1968

Innate Mechanisms, Rearing Conditions, and a Theory of Early Experience Effects in Primates[1]

GENE P. SACKETT
University of Wisconsin

THE PURPOSE of this paper is to review selected studies in rhesus monkeys that suggest hypotheses concerning mechanisms underlying behavioral development. The experimental data deal with innate information processing functions in primates, and the persistence into adulthood of effects produced by variations in social and nonsocial stimulation. The introductory section presents an outline for a framework of animal development research, a classification of research problems involving genetic and early postnatal variables, and a restatement (e.g., King, 1958) of several methodological and definitional problems in interpreting early experience effects. Also, the term *development* will be defined, implications of this definition for validly testing and explaining early experience effects will be discussed, and several current explanations of early experience effects will be briefly summarized.

1. I would like to expess my thanks to Drs. Harry F. and Margaret K. Harlow and the students and associates at the University of Wisconsin Primate Laboratories. Their experimental studies form an important part of this paper, and some of their ideas concerning primate behavioral development provided a major stimulus for my own notions. Also, I would like to thank Mr. Charles Pratt and Dr. Dennis Clark for the long hours of argument, discussion, and analysis that led to many of the experiments and hypotheses presented here. Grant MH-11894 from the National Institute of Mental Health supported most of the studies presented in this paper and partially supported manuscript preparation.

INTRODUCTION

Potential sources of variation between individuals in adult behavior include genetic, prenatal, perinatal, neonatal, infantile, and preadult factors. A developmental explanation of this variability might proceed by estimating the proportion of total variance contributed by treatments imposed at these different developmental levels. Animal research suggests that within a species genetic factors limit this range of variability, while prenatal and postnatal treatments increase variability in the willingness or capacity of individuals to interact in a changing environment. Postnatal research suggests that differences in rearing conditions can alter the distribution of measures involving social, emotional, exploratory, and perceptual behaviors, as well as performance on learning and intellectual tasks.

Genetic Factors

Genetic experiments have been concerned with at least two basic problems. The first involves behavioral constancy produced by selective breeding (e.g., Scudder, Karczmar, & Lockett, 1967). Such experiments permit identification of behaviors that have important genetic controls, estimation of the number of genes involved, and when coupled with prenatal or postnatal treatments allow estimation of the relative vulnerability of a behavior to nongenetic modification. A second class of studies more directly related to this paper involves identification of unlearned mechanisms, sometimes called fixed action patterns, producing within-species behavioral constancy (e.g., Thorpe, 1963). Behaviorally, such studies involve specifying stimuli, or relations among stimuli, that release a specific response, or class of responses, in the absence of prior learning and reinforcement. Unlearned behaviors, such as differential visual fixation by human neonates of stimuli varying in complexity (e.g., Fantz, 1961), may be present at birth or hatching. Other unlearned responses, such as the initial release of following by birds during imprinting, may require postnatal maturation of sensory, motor, or emotional systems before emerging in behavior.

As a basic axiom of learning, it might be stated that primary conditioning is built on relations between input and response that are standard unlearned equipment. Classical conditioning theory thus requires the presence of unconditioned S-R connections before learning can occur, and instrumental conditioning theories require the presence of operant responses released or elicited by any stimulus as necessary for learning. It seems surprising, therefore, that experimenting psychologists have largely ignored mechanisms providing innate biases for attending to the stimuli that release the behaviors necessary for learning. This seems especially true in the study of higher mammals and primates, where it is often assumed that innate mechanisms other than reflexes play a minor role in behavioral development (e.g., Morgan & King, 1966, p. 41).

Postnatal Factors

Studies of early experience effects on later behavior have included a variety of manipulations, measures, and identifications for the terms "early" and "later" within the life span of the subject. Many of the manipulations involve variations in rearing conditions. These can be classified into several categories: sensory and social isolation, involving reduction from control levels in the quality and quantity of available stimulation and response opportunities; gross stimulus enrichment above control levels; systematic enrichment and deprivation of specific inputs, other stimuli remaining the same as in a control condition; stress conditions such as handling, temperature changes, or intense input of any type; and "maternal" variation involving differences in input afforded a neonate by its caretaker.

For some investigators "early" experience begins at, or shortly after, birth (e.g., Harlow & Harlow, 1966); for others "early" commences at weaning (e.g., Fuller, 1967) or some later developmental event. This often ignored discrepancy in temporal onset of treatments produces difficulty in interpreting and generalizing effects both within and between species—difficulty that is particularly acute in identifying and explaining critical or sensitive period effects. For example, certain critical experiences imposed before weaning may be necessary for the actual appearance of a response in the subsequent behavioral repertoire (i.e., critical period), or this preweaning experience may be necessary for reaching the same quantitative response levels as control subjects (i.e., sensitive period). Also, preweaning treatments may have persistent later effects, while the same treatment imposed after weaning may have only transitory effects, or no effects at all. This implies that valid comparisons of a treatment effect between species and between laboratories must involve the application of treatments at similar maturational stages.

The term "later" has also referred to a variety of developmental periods. Some studies conduct criterion tests immediately after rearing, and thus examine the effects of early experience on early behavior. Other studies measure persistence of effects by retesting at different points in development or by testing at adult maturation. Although the effects of early treatments on early behavior can certainly be of interest, such effects seem important only when they persist into adult behavior or interact with postrearing experience to produce effects on adult behavior.

A Criterion for Testing Rearing Effects

The term development means a process of change. The viewpoint of this paper is that behavioral development is identified by increases in the ability and willingness of an individual to respond appropriately to stimulus changes in the social and nonsocial environment. These stimulus changes, interacting with physical maturation, place new demands on the developing individual's behavioral capacities. Conceptually, developmental changes in ability or willingness may involve (1) the performance of innate or previously learned responses to new or modified stimuli; (2) the inhibition or modification of previously performed responses, or the acquisition of new responses to familiar stimuli; or (3) a combination involving response change to changed stimuli.

According to this view behavioral development cannot be demonstrated under static conditions. Adequate and valid developmental tests must involve a discrepancy between the stimuli to which the individual has been adapted and/or the responses that it has made previously, and the stimulus and/or response demands imposed by the current stimulus situation. This implies that early experience effects involving response to the external environment cannot be assessed in the rearing situation. Criterion tests must proceed under conditions that offer some degree of quantitative or qualitative change from the rearing input. Following from this analysis, a basic goal of early experience research is specification of the rearing conditions necessary to yield individuals who can adapt to changed stimulation as they advance into adulthood.

Explanations of Early Experience Effects

Four general views seem to be common in explaining early experience effects.

Atrophy. Severe deprivation during rearing of input in specific modalities such as vision and audition has produced structural and biochemical degeneration in sensory systems (e.g., Riesen, 1960; Gyllensten, Malmfors, & Norrlin, 1966). This suggests that deprivation rearing may produce later behavioral deficits due to physical atrophy of mechanisms that were mature at birth or shortly after.

Developmental Failure and Potentiation. A related view involves mechanisms that are either undeveloped or only partially developed at birth, and that require postnatal sensory input for full maturation (e.g., Fox, 1966). Environments void of certain critical inputs may produce later deficits because the physiological substrate underlying a response or information processing function fails to mature. Conversely, stimulus enrichment may increase the rate or quality of maturation of some responses by potentiating structural or biochemical growth (e.g., Rosenzweig, 1966). Enriched rearing thus could permanently increase the quality or quantity of behaviors related to maturationally potentiated physiological systems.

Learning Deficits. A third explanation suggests that deficits are caused by failure of the early environment to provide experiences critical for basic perceptual-motor development. A failure to learn to organize and integrate perceptual and motor responses early in life may thus permanently lower ability to adapt to change (e.g., Hebb, 1949).

Emergence Trauma. A final explanation assumes that deficits are a function of discrepancies in the quality or quantity of stimulation between rearing and testing environments (e.g., Fuller, 1967). When large, such discrepancies may produce high arousal or emotionality, resulting in fear and disturbance, disorientation, hyperactivity, or avoidance. Early experience effects are thus viewed as emotional deficits produced by the interaction of rearing and test stimulation levels, rather than specific deficits in learning, perception, or neurochemical processes. Accordingly, deficits should be minimal or absent if emergence trauma is controlled by a paced schedule of postrearing changes in stimulus novelty, intensity, and complexity.

In view of the criteria presented above for assessing effects, the emergence trauma view actually seems to be descriptive rather than explanatory. The occurrence of heightened emotionality under changed conditions does not explain why the rearing treatment produced an animal that reacts emotionally in the face of change—the change imposed on the animal merely serves as a necessary procedure for assessing the effect of the rearing experience. This is not to deny that postrearing variables do interact with rearing experiences, but the fact of interaction does not explain the effect.

INNATE MECHANISMS IN PRIMATE BEHAVIOR

The research summarized in this section concerns identification of innate functions in social choice and social communication. Several studies were conducted in a free-choice situation that allows monkeys to select among social stimuli by making differential approach or bodily orientation responses. Figure 1 presents a schematic drawing of this self-selection circus apparatus. The unit is constructed of aluminum channels, bolted to aluminum forms, forming a hexagonal outer perime-

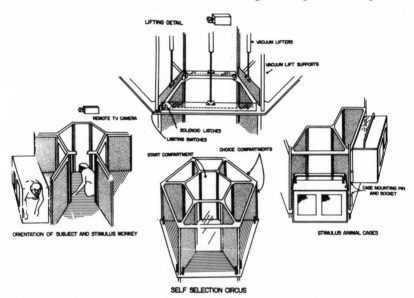

FIG.1. The circus apparatus used to study social preferences. (Lower center) Center start compartment and choice compartments: the stippled choice compartment walls were opaque Masonite; the front and inner walls were clear Plexiglas, indicated by slashes. (Upper center) Vacuum cylinder door lifts, position of TV camera, solenoid latches that locked the walls so they could not be raised by the subject, and limit switches that operated a light indicating proper functioning of the vacuum lifters. (Right) Mounting brackets, and aluminum stimulus animal cages with clear Plexiglas on the front and one half of the top section. (Left) The relative position of a stimulus and subject monkey during the exposure period.

ter. Six choice compartments surround the inner start compartment and are separated from the start compartment by vertically sliding walls. Opaque walls block access to unused compartments. Each of the seven stainless steel rod floor sections is electrically isolated and wired into a contact circuit that operates clocks, recording time in the compartment when a monkey steps on the floor. Vacuum lifts raise the doors separating start from choice compartments. A stimulus animal cage is hooked onto the outside of the choice compartments, allowing an unobstructed view of stimulus monkeys from start or choice compartments.

In the standard test procedure specific types of monkeys are randomly assigned to stimulus animal cages. The subject is placed in the start compartment with the inner Plexiglas doors that separate the start compartment from the choice compartments closed. During a 5-minute exposure period the subject can see and hear the stimulus monkeys but cannot enter the choice compartments. The inner doors are then raised for a 10-minute choice period, during which the subject can enter and reenter any choice compartment or can remain in the center. In the choice compartment the subject has close visual and auditory contact with the stimulus animal, but physical interaction is not possible. In addition to the time spent in each choice compartment, an observer records duration of bodily orientation, scored whenever the subject orients its head and body toward a given stimulus animal, regardless of the choice compartment the subject is in.

Own-Species Preference

A study measuring preference for own-species over other macaque species suggested effects of innate factors in social attachment behavior (Sackett, Suomi, & Grady, 1968). Three types of feral-born adult females (Figure 2) served as stimulus animals in the circus: namely, (1) a rhesus (*Macaca mulatta*), (2) a pig-tail (*Macaca nemestrina*), and (3) a stump-tail (*Macaca speciosa*). In most respects the rhesus and pig-tail are more alike physically than is either to the stump-tail.

In one social preference test feral-born adult rhesus, stump-tail, and pig-tail macaques served as subjects. Each animal received one trial, measuring duration of compartment entry and bodily orientation toward each stimulus animal. The data are shown in Figure 3. Regardless of the sex of the subject, each species preferred the female stimulus animal of its own species as measured by either entry duration ($p < .001$) or

FIG. 2. Adult female stimulus animals used in the species preference experiment, and a 30-day-old rhesus monkey. (Upper right, rhesus; upper left, pig-tail; lower left, stump-tail.)

bodily orientation ($p < .02$). These data thus validate the circus technique as an indicator of social preference and suggest that the two measures, although differing in absolute values, reflect the same basic relationships.

In another preference test conducted under identical conditions, monkeys ranging in age from 1 to 9 months had been separated from their mothers shortly after birth. These partial isolates lived alone in bare

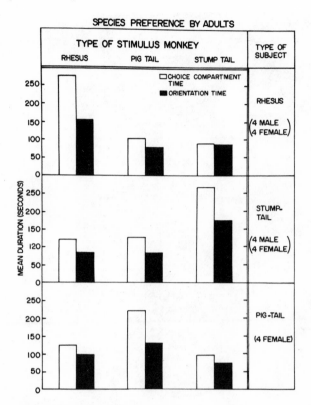

FIG. 3. Preferences by adult feral-born rhesus, stump-tail, and pig-tail subjects for adult females of the same and the other species.

wire cages (Figure 4) from which age-mates could be seen and heard, but not touched. After maternal separation the subjects had neither visual nor auditory contact with monkeys other than age-mates.

Subjects under 7 months of age rarely entered choice compartments, perhaps because of excessive fear or motor inabilities; therefore, only orientation data are presented. The results shown in Table 1 reveal that rhesus infants at all ages, including those between 1 to 2 months, preferred the adult rhesus female over the pig-tail and stump-tail ferals.

There is a great difference in physical appearance between infant rhesus monkeys and any of the three types of adult female stimulus animals (Figure 2). It seems unlikely that neonates separated from

Fɪɢ. 4. Partial isolation cages from which the monkey could see and hear, but not touch, other animals.

mothers at birth, and having visual and auditory contact only with other neonates, have learned cues enabling them to discriminate an adult female rhesus from the other species. These data suggest, therefore, that this preference for own-species may be based on specific unlearned cues involving the physical appearance of the female, her vocalizations, or motor patterns such as retrieval gestures that are unique to rhesus females. Such unlearned, prepotent stimuli could play an important role in the development of social attachments.

TABLE 1

Orientation Measures by Age

AGE (months)	SAMPLE SIZE		ORIENTATION TIME (seconds)			HIGHEST SCORE			p
	M	F	Rhesus	Pig-Tail	Stump-Tail	Rhesus	Pig-Tail	Stump-Tail	
1–2	4	4	70	45	12	6	2	0	.039
3–4	4	4	118	40	36	7	1	0	.005
7–9	6	4	127	76	55	7	2	1	.039

Note: Mean orientation time by partial isolates of three ages toward an adult rhesus, pig-tail, and stump-tail female in the circus. Data are also given for the number of subjects at each age having their highest orientation time toward each stimulus alternative. The p values for this measure were calculated from two-tailed binomial tests with $P = \frac{1}{3}$, $Q = \frac{2}{3}$. F tests showed significant effects of stimulus type at each age (all $p. < .001$) on the orientation time measure, with no sex x stimulus interactions (all $p > .05$).

Female versus Male Preference

Male and female rhesus monkeys between the ages of 2 to 10 months, and adults (> 54 months) who had been separated from their mothers at birth and reared under the partial isolation conditions described in the previous study, were given a choice between an adult feral male and female rhesus monkey in the circus (Suomi, 1968). Duration of orientation scores are presented in Table 2. All eight male and eight female subjects under 11 months of age had higher durations of orienting toward the female stimulus animal. Adults preferred their own sex. This indicates that even in the absence of early postnatal experience with adult animals, an adult female is preferred over an adult male by neonates and infants; again suggesting the presence of an unlearned bias to approach a specific type of social stimulus.

Auditory Reactivity by Neonates

Mother-infant interactions in rhesus monkeys are characterized by intimate physical contact and maternal protection. Disturbances in the environment or by the baby monkey generally result in retrieval behaviors by the mother. Vocalizations such as barks and growls are employed by the mother as one type of signal warning the infant to return. The following study suggested that neonatal responses to maternal calls may

Gene P. Sackett

TABLE 2
Orientation Toward Adult Male and Adult Female

AGE (months)	SEX	SIZE SAMPLE	SECONDS OF ORIENTATION	
			Adult Male	Adult Female
2–3	M	2	4	36
	F	2	18	101
4	M	2	12	84
	F	2	6	308
6–7	M	2	52	156
	F	2	5	31
9–10	M	2	25	84
	F	2	19	86
Adult	M	6	158	76
	F	6	56	136

Note: Mean duration of orientation (seconds) in the circus toward an adult male and an adult female feral-born rhesus stimulus animal. Data are given for partial isolates under 11 months of age, and for adult partial isolates who had intensive social experience after year one. All 16 infants had their highest orientation toward the adult female, while all six adult male and six female partial isolates had their highest orientation toward the stimulus animal of their own sex.

be unlearned, resulting from a genetically tuned mechanism (Sackett & Tripp, 1968).

Four male and four female monkeys were separated from their mothers immediately after birth, and reared in individual cages with no opportunities to hear vocalizations from adult monkeys, although they could see and hear each other. Shortly after birth two males and two females received injections of radioactive iodine 131. This isotope selectively destroys the thyroid gland, producing hypothyroid animals whose skeletal, endocrine, and neural development are seriously retarded by 60 days of age.

At 30 days tests for auditory reactivity were initiated in a small chamber placed in a sound-isolated room. Closed-circuit TV allowed an observer to view and score the subject's behavior. Each subject received 7 days of testing with pure tone frequencies of .5, 1, 2, 3, and 5 kHz at sound pressure levels of 40, 55, and 70 db (low, medium, and loud intensities). Individual trials consisted of a 15-second prestimulus period, a 15-second stimulation period, and a 15-second poststimulus period. Control trials were also run on which tones were omitted. Each individual frequency occurred seven times at each intensity, yielding a total of 21 presentations.

The response measure was occurrence of a behavioral change within 2 seconds after tone onset. Behavioral changes were defined as any alterations in motor behavior, vocalization, or both. For example, if the subject was active or vocalizing during the prestimulus period, then became inactive or stopped vocalizing within 2 seconds after tone onset, a behavior change was scored. Conversely, if the subject was inactive or silent and then became active or vocalized after tone onset a change was also scored.

The results were analyzed in terms of the probability of a behavioral change for each frequency-intensity combination. On 112 soundless control trials there were no behavioral changes. This compared with an average probability of .32 for all sound trials. Pure tones, therefore, did influence the behavior of one-month-old monkeys.

Analysis of variance revealed no significant difference between control and hypothyroid subjects averaged over frequency and intensity ($p >$ .05). Overall reactivity to sound did not differ between the groups. Although louder tones increased behavioral change probabilities, there was no interaction between intensity and frequency ($p > .05$). The group x frequency interaction, however, shown in Figure 5, was significant ($p < .005$). Maximal reactivity occurred at .5 and 5 kHz for the normal monkeys, and at 1 kHz for the hypothyroids. Subsequent t tests (all $p < .05$) showed that .5 and 5 kHz were significantly higher in behavioral change probability than 1 and 3 kHz, which were higher than 2 kHz for the controls. For the hypothyroids, 1 kHz was higher than all other tones, which did not differ from each other.

The potential significance of these data was suggested by sound spectograms of adult female and neonate rhesus vocalizations made by Mr. Anthony Marmarou of the Franklin Institute, Philadelphia. Analysis revealed that sound energy densities occurring in a band between 250–500 Hz and in a band between 4,500–5,000 Hz were more probable for adult females than any other frequencies in the range 50–10,000 Hz. Vocalizations of neonates did not exhibit these properties, containing

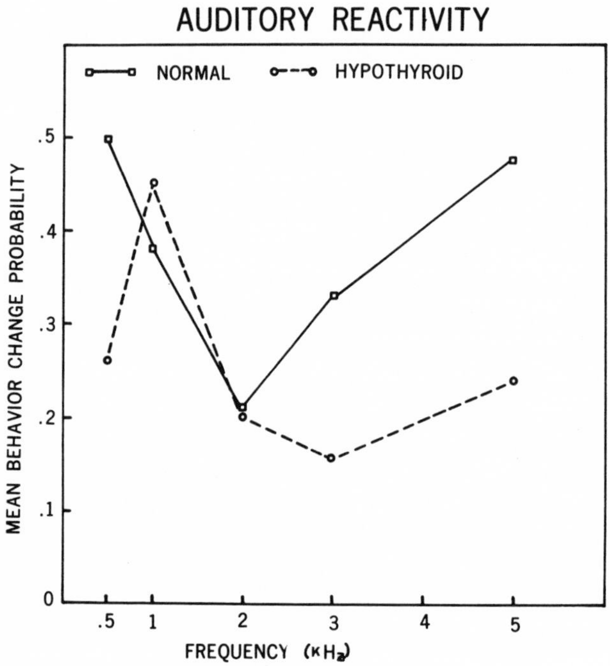

AUDITORY REACTIVITY

FIG. 5. The probability of a behavioral change at tone onset as a function of pure tone frequency for physiologically normal and hypothyroid 30-day old monkeys.

more energy in the middle and higher frequencies. Similar results were obtained by Rowell and Hinde (1962) in analysis of adult rhesus barks, growls, and squeaks, with frequencies of 200–500 and 4,000–5,000 Hz appearing to predominate. The facts seem to indicate that (1) vocalizations of adult female rhesus monkeys contain a large portion of their sound energy in the ranges 250–500 and 4,000–5,000 Hz, (2) physiologically normal neonates are maximally reactive to tones at 500 and 5,000 Hz, while (3) developmentally damaged hypothyroids show a frequency shift to maximal reactivity at 1 kHz. The following conclusions, although highly speculative, seem consistent with these correlations.

It is suggested that at birth or soon after rhesus monkeys possess a tuned auditory mechanism that produces maximal responsiveness to the vocalizations of adult females. The neonate thus does not have to learn to respond to the mother's vocalizations—the auditory system is prewired for these sounds. The fact that hypothyroids did not show the same frequency function as controls, although they were not different in overall auditory reactivity, suggests that this "auditory releasing mechanism" either develops postnatally, or is present at birth but atrophies due to abnormalities related to the thyroxin deficiency.

Innate Mechanisms in Social Communication

A final experiment in this section concerns monkeys reared in total social isolation with opportunity to respond to colored slides projected on the rear of the cage (Sackett, 1966). These "picture isolates" were removed from their mothers within 24 hours after birth and placed in totally enclosed cages. Throughout the 9-month rearing period each of the four male and four female subjects was exposed to a variety of pictures including threatening, playing, fearful, withdrawing, and sexing monkeys as well as pictures of infants, mother and infant together, and monkeys doing "nothing." Control pictures included humans, landscapes, buildings, and geometric patterns. Except for the pictures, and an initial 2-week period of hand-feeding on a wire rack, no other sources of varied visual input or contact with real monkeys or humans were available.

Three general effects characterized the responses of these isolates to the pictures. After the first 30 days pictures containing monkeys generally received more exploration and play than nonmonkey pictures; and pictures of infants and of monkeys displaying threat produced more exploratory and play responses and higher motor activity than any other type of picture. No pictures produced fear, withdrawal, or disturbance behaviors until about day 80. From days 80 to 120 the frequencies of these behaviors rose markedly for all subjects whenever threat pictures were presented, even though these stimuli had not produced fear and disturbance before this time. Subsequently the frequency of fear to threat stimuli declined, but remained higher than for other pictures throughout rearing. These effects of threat stimuli on fear and disturbance can be seen in Figure 6.

These data suggested several conclusions. First, two kinds of socially meaningful visual stimuli, pictures of infants and of monkeys threatening, seem to have unlearned, prepotent, activating properties for socially naïve monkeys. Second, visual components of threat displays appear to function as innate releasers of fear, and this innate mechanism seems to

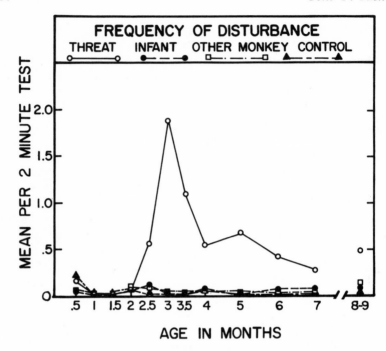

FIG. 6. Frequency of fear and disturbance behaviors by picture isolates when pictures of monkeys threatening, infants, all other types of monkey stimuli, and control stimuli were presented in the isolation cage during the 9-month rearing period.

require postnatal maturation before becoming operative. At least certain aspects of complex social communication in primates may lie in innate recognition and response mechanisms, rather than in social learning during interactions with species members.

The studies reviewed in this section suggest that in primates, as in lower vertebrates and invertebrates, innate information processing mechanisms may play a major role in development. These mechanisms may influence such complex behaviors as species recognition, social stimulus preferences leading to attachment formation, and social communication behaviors. Inborn receptive, analyzing, and reaction systems may thus provide important building blocks for social learning. The next section of this paper reviews experiments on rearing effects that persist into preadult and adult behavior.

REARING CONDITIONS AND DEVELOPMENT

Rhesus monkeys studied at the Wisconsin Primate Laboratories received neonatal (birth-2 months) and infantile (2–12 months) experiences in the cities and forests of Southeast Asia (feral), or in laboratory situations containing mothers and peers, mothers or peers only, inanimate surrogate mothers, visual and auditory but not physical peer contact, or complete privation from maternal and peer contact in an unchanging perceptual world. On tests of motor activity, exploration, social affiliation and play, and intellectual performance, animals raised with mother and/or peer contact have not differed in any important respects; and where laboratory comparisons are available, did not differ markedly from feral monkeys. This work has been reviewed in several places (e.g., Harlow & Harlow, 1966; Harlow, Schiltz, & Harlow, 1968; Sackett, 1968a) and will not be emphasized here. The data to be presented concern effects of three rearing conditions, motherless mothering, partial isolation, and total isolation compared with feral, feral-mothered, and peer-only control conditions.

Motherless-mothered (MM) neonates were those reared by females who were themselves deprived of maternal and peer contact during infancy (Harlow & Seay, 1966). The basic rearing situation was a "playpen" apparatus where four mother-infant pairs lived in individual cages (Figure 7). The infants received daily peer interaction in a central play area that could not be entered by the mother. Control animals were reared by feral-born mothers (FM) under the same conditions.

In partial isolation (PI) animals lived for the first 6 to 12 months in bare wire cages from which other monkeys could be seen and heard, but opportunity for physical interaction was unavailable (Figure 4). These infants were separated from their mothers at birth, spent the first month being hand-fed, then lived together in cages with age-mates for 8 to 12 months.

Total isolates were reared in completely enclosed cages (Figure 7). The isolate could see itself, food, and the cage walls and could hear some outside noises, but there were no varied sources of visual, tactual, or proprioceptive input other than self-produced stimuli. Early isolation commenced immediately after birth, and was studied for 3, 6, 9, and 12 month durations. Late isolation, in which the neonate lived in partial isolation with or without limited peer interaction before isolation started, was studied from 3 to 9 and 6 to 12 months of age.

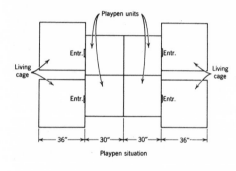
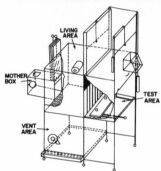

FIG. 7. Pictures and schematic drawings of the playpen (left) and total isolation (right) rearing conditions. In the playpen, pairs of mothers and infants interact in the wire mesh living cages, while infants can play with each other and toys in the play area. In isolation, the infant lives in the middle area after spending the first 30 days in the "mother box," being hand-fed through portholes. The front area contains equipment for studying development of discrimination learning. The inside of the totally enclosed apparatus is gray sheet metal, with a lighted ceiling and a fan for air circulation.

TWO EFFECTS OF VERY EARLY EXPERIENCE

Motherless Mothering

Females reared in partial isolation or on surrogate mothers were either indifferent or brutal with their first offspring (Arling & Harlow, 1968). Indifferent MMs generally ignored their babies during the first 2 to 3 months, rarely nursed, and had reduced amounts of physical contact with the infant compared with FMs. In addition to these behaviors, brutal MMs inflicted severe physical punishment including bites, cuffs, and grinding the infant into the wire floor. Most MM infants required supplemental feeding to survive. A characteristic behavior of MM infants involved repeated attempts to contact the mother that were ofen met with rejection by pushing the infant away, or physical attacks. Even though repeatedly rejected or punished, these infants failed to inhibit approach and grasping responses. By the second or third month this persistence often resulted in the mother's capitulation, allowing the infant to maintain physical contact.

In the playpen situation FMs showed almost no physical rejection during the first month (Figure 8). At about 4 months, FMs began rejecting their infants, pushing them away when the infant initiated physical contact. This "separation" process seems to be a normal part of mother-

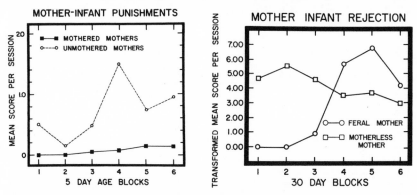

FIG. 8. Differences between mothered (feral-born) and unmothered (laboratory-reared) monkeys in physical punishment toward their first baby (left graph) during the first month, and in rejection of the baby by pushing it away from the mother's body (right graph) during the first six months of playpen rearing. Note that feral mothers increase rejection behaviors during a "separation" period between months 4 to 6, while motherless mothers maintain a constant level of rejection during this time.

ing in rhesus monkeys (Harlow, Harlow, & Hansen, 1963) and results in increased exploratory behavior and peer contact by the infants. This separation process did not occur in MMs. One major difference between MM and FM rearing, therefore, was in the age at which infants were rejected. The MM offspring received rejection during the first 2 to 3 months—an age at which clasping and grasping reflexes, and "contact comfort" motives are at high levels. Their repeated attempts to initiate contact suggests that these are also ages at which monkeys are unable to inhibit approach and grasp-clasp responses. Offspring of FMs received rejection at ages when inhibition of approach behavior no longer competed strongly with grasping and clasping reflexes, or with high motivation for contact comfort. This difference in the opportunity and ability for learning inhibitory responses may play a crucial role in the major behavioral abnormality of MM offspring to be discussed next.

The development of exploratory and social behaviors of MM compared with FM offspring appeared identical except in two respects (Arling & Harlow, 1968). Lower levels of infantile sexual behavior and higher levels of contact initiation and aggression appeared in MM offspring. Follow-up studies of MM offspring at 3 and 4 years of age (Mitchell, Arling & Møller, 1967; Sackett, 1967b) indicated that hyper-aggression persisted into preadulthood. In pairings with strangers the offspring of MMs exhibited higher levels of physical aggression than monkeys reared under any other laboratory conditions (see Table 3).

TABLE 3

Effects of Varied Early Experience on Later Social Interaction

MEASURE	GROUP					
	1YI	6ME	PI	FM	MM	F RATIO
Physical Contact	3.1	3.4	8.5	16.6	32.4	3.71*
Aggression	6.8	4.2	5.6	10.2	27.5	5.25*
Fear-Withdrawal	97	25	34	12	6	5.74*
Motor Activity	86	121	117	229	203	7.32**

*$p < .05$;   **$p < .01$

Note: Effects of varied experience during year 1 on social interaction at 4 years of age. One year (1YI) and 6-month (6ME) early total isolates, partial isolates (PI), feral-mothered (FM), and motherless-mothered (MM) monkeys were paired in a wire cage with unfamiliar male and female age-mate partners. The data are durations, in seconds, averaged over 10-minute tests with each type of partner, of (1) physical contact initiated by the subject, (2) threat and physical attack on the stranger, (3) fear and withdrawal from the stranger, and time locomoting in space. F tests for group effects have $df = 4/22$.

The MM offspring were rarely brutalized after 2 to 3 months. In fact, (Figure 8) after the third month these monkeys received less rejection than FM infants. This suggests that experience during months 3 to 6 is critically involved in the expression of aggression by rhesus monkeys.

It was previously suggested that specific responses leading to later hyper-aggression in MM offspring were learned by observing and interacting with rejecting and brutal mothers during the first 3 months of life (Sackett, 1968). Rather than early learning (modeling) of behaviors specific to aggression, however, it seems plausible that the persistent hyperaggression of MM offspring may be due to a general deficit in the ability to inhibit intense responses. As outlined earlier, the behavior of normally mothered rhesus neonates is almost completely controlled by the mother during the first months; many attempts to change position or to leave the mother are inhibited. Conversely, during the separation period at 4 to 5 months the FM infants learn to inhibit approach responses to the mother as the result of her rejection. Such inhibitory training is not effective in MM offspring, who despite punishment make repeated and eventually successful attempts to attain contact with their mothers, and do not experience the separation stage of development. This failure to learn to inhibit approach and contact initiation responses during months 3 to 6 could form the basis for later failure to inhibit aggression and intense contact behaviors by MM offspring.

Preadult Choice Behavior

Animals reared under a variety of conditions were tested in the circus (Figure 1) for preference between a monkey and an adult human female (Sackett, Porter, & Holmes, 1965). All subjects were between 3.5 and 4.5 years when tested, and had received intensive social experience with monkeys after the first year. In testing, a 5-minute exposure and a 5-minute test trial were given. The stimulus monkeys were the same age and sex as the subjects.

The results, shown in Table 4, revealed that (1) partial isolates, who had intimate human contact during the first month and then lived in individual cages for the rest of year 1, preferred the human female; (2) peer-only subjects, who also received early human contact but lived with other monkeys after the first 30 days, preferred the monkey stimulus, as did mother-peer raised animals who had no early human contact; and (3) total isolates, who received neither human nor monkey contact during the first 6 or 12 months, preferred the center area, a position maximally distant from either stimulus.

These data show that specific experience with a human during the first 30 days of life can affect choice for a social stimulus 3 to 4 years later.

TABLE 4

Effects of Early Experience on Later Preferences

REARING CONDITION	n	CHOICE COMPARTMENT		
		Female	Monkey	Area
Partial Isolate	7	226	36	38
Peer-Only	12	27	165	108
Mother-Peer	12	11	191	98
6-Month¹ Isolate	4	4	99	197
1-Year Isolate	4	0	126	174

Note: Mean choice compartment entry time (seconds) in circus tests with a human versus an age-mate monkey as stimuli. The compartment having the maximum choice time was significantly greater than the other two compartments for each group (all $p < .01$).

Having contact with monkeys immediately after the first month alters this effect, however, while a total lack of contact with monkeys or humans during the first 6 months appears to produce a permanent decrement in degree of preference for monkeys. This suggests that experience during the first 6 months may be crucial for forming social attachments in rhesus monkeys. Data on the adequacy of social behavior in partial and total isolates supports this contention.

Effects of Partial Isolation

Long-term PI effects on home-cage behavior—the environment to which the monkey is fully adapted—were found by Cross and Harlow (1965) in comparing 1 to 7 year old PIs with mother-peer controls. Even in the home cage PIs showed more stereotyped pacing, rocking, and huddling responses, self-orality, and disturbance. When presented with a fear stimulus all subjects showed disturbance and aggression; however, controls directed threat toward the object or the experimenter, while PIs physically attacked themselves with vigorous self-bites that sometimes resulted in physical wounds. Older PIs exhibited bizarre idiosyncratic responses in which the animal's arm or leg moved slowly upward, was visually fixated, grabbed, and jerked down or violently mauled. Rearing without physical peer contact thus produced abnormal motor patterns, disturbance, and inability to appropriately direct aggression and threat. The fact that these abnormal behaviors occurred in the home cage suggests that some abnormal effects of deprivation rearing do not depend on emergence trauma involving emotional responses induced by rearing-test environment discrepancies.

Long-term effects of PI on nonsocial and social behaviors have been studied in several other experiments. In one situation subjects were exposed to male and female strangers in a small cage (Sackett, 1967b). Compared with mother-peer controls (Table 3) deficits were present in motor activity, physical contact initiation, and aggression, while fear behavior was heightened. Other data revealed that compared to feral or mother-peer raised monkeys PIs were deficient in exploratory behavior, evidenced by long latencies to enter a novel environment, preference for visual patterns lower in complexity, and failure to interact with complex movement-producing stimuli (Sackett, 1965a, 1965b).

As with maternal behavior, the sexual behavior of PIs was grossly inadequate (Harlow, Joslyn, Senko, & Dopp, 1966). When paired with sexually sophisticated partners, both male and female PIs were hyper-aggressive, had low amounts of grooming and social proximity, high levels of self-clutching and self-biting, and few appropriate sexual motor responses. After experience with sophisticated males, many female PIs improved in sexual responding and became impregnated. Male PIs, although highly aroused, never became sexually adequate and failed to produce offspring after home-cage pairings with sexually receptive feral females.

The PI monkeys in these studies all received social and nonsocial experience after the first year of life. The persistence of behavioral deficits, even after extensive "therapy" experiences, suggests that rearing without physical peer contact produced animals unable to adapt adequately to many social and nonsocial situations. In situations requiring approach behaviors toward inanimate objects and physical contact with other monkeys, characteristic behavior involving stereotyped movements, self-aggression, and self-clutching occurred at high levels. This suggests that one major deficit produced by PI rearing lies in inability to inhibit earlier learned or innate responses that have a high probability of occurrence in all situations including the home cage; these responses compete with the behaviors required for adequate adjustment to social and nonsocial stimulus changes. In particular, these behaviors compete with initiating and maintaining physical contact with other monkeys—a prerequisite for adequate social, sexual, and maternal behavior.

Effects of Total Isolation

Studies of total social isolation reveal striking and persistent behavioral anomalies. Rowland (1964) studied 6-month (6ME), 12-month (1Y) early, and 6-month late (6ML) isolates, paired with PI controls in a playroom immediately after the end of isolation. These data show that (1) one year in isolation devastated positive social responding, motor activity, and exploration, with most of the time in the playroom spent in self-clutching, rocking, and huddling. (2) After 32 weeks of daily playroom tests, 6ME subjects were still lower than PI controls on most behaviors, but had increased in play and exploration, and decreased in disturbance, withdrawal, and fear. (3) 6ML isolates, who spent their first 6 months in partial isolation, were hyperactive and hyperaggressive, engaging in play and exploration at higher levels than PI controls. Many of the 6ML behaviors consisted of violent attacks, rarely observed in other 1 year old animals, on their PI partners; therefore, differences in 6ML and PI behavior may have been due more to fear of attack by the controls than actual differences in social competence.

One striking abnormality appeared in the 1-year isolates. Control animals sometimes aggressed against these isolates by biting and pulling out fur. The isolates failed to exhibit escape or avoidance behaviors, and often showed no overt reaction to stimuli that are painful to normal monkeys. This suggests that, as with dogs (Melzack & Scott, 1957), extreme isolation produced deficits in the ability of monkeys to sense, or react appropriately, to noxious stimulation.

Griffin and Harlow (1966) studied the consequences of 3 months in early isolation (3ME) for playroom behavior between months 4 to 9. After an initial postisolation depression, involving low motor activity and failure to eat, the 3ME isolates did not differ from PI controls in any respect. When compared with PI controls, 3 months of early isolation did not produce deficits in behavior, whereas 6 or 12 months of early isolation did produce anomalies in postrearing behavior. Six months of late isolation in the first year also affected behavior, but these effects involved hyperactivity and aggression rather than depressed exploratory and social behavior. The first 6 months of life thus appear to be a sensitive period for later social and nonsocial development.

One criticism of these interpretations concerns the emergence trauma notion that deficits resulted from emotional responses when the isolates were thrust into the complex playroom environment. To study this problem, Clark (1968) assessed the effects of 6 months in isolation given immediately after birth (6ME), between months 3 to 9 (6MI), and during the second 6 months of life (6ML). To reduce emergence effects, during isolation all subjects received nonsocial adaptation to the playroom during the 6 months of the first year not spent in isolation. During this 6 months of nonisolation, the subjects lived in wire cages. Control subjects lived in wire cages and received social and nonsocial playroom adaptation spread throughout the first year.

During and immediately after isolation, differences were observed in disturbance behavior involving rocking, crouching, self-clutching, and huddling (Figure 9). Animals isolated at birth developed higher levels

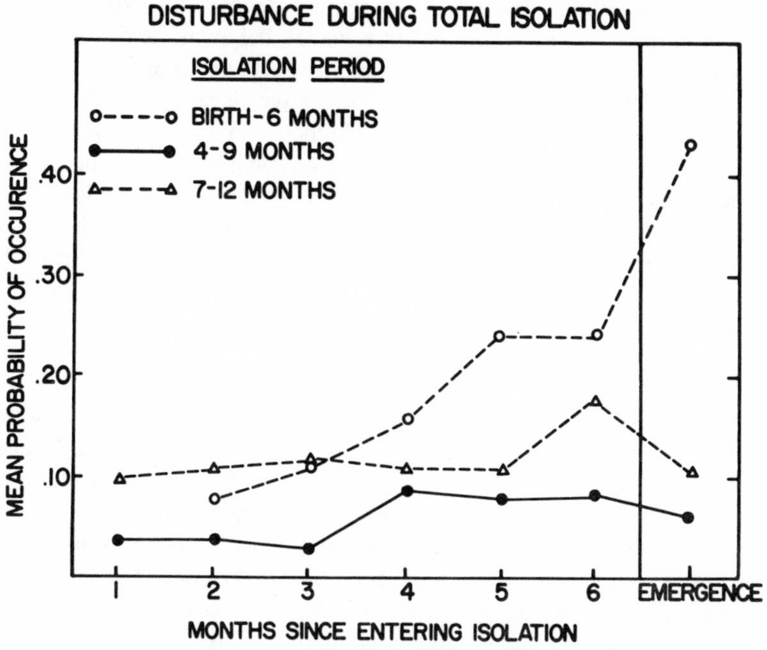

FIG. 9. Disturbance behaviors for animals isolated at different 6 month periods during the first year of life, and during the first month after emergence from isolation into wire cages. The data show the relative frequency of disturbance out of the total frequency of all behaviors during daily observation periods.

of these behaviors than animals isolated at 3 or 6 months. On emergence from isolation the early isolates increased in disturbance while the other groups decreased. In playroom criterion tests between 12 to 15 months of age the early isolates were withdrawn, fearful, inactive, and deficient in play and exploratory behavior compared with controls. Follow-up tests conducted at 24 months paired all subjects with mother-peer controls. All three isolate groups and the wire-cage controls were deficient in positive social behaviors involving affiliation, play, sex, and exploration. The 6ME and 3ML isolates exhibited intense physical contact including aggression not seen in 6ML, wire-cage, or mother-peer monkeys. All of the isolation conditions and partial isolation thus had produced typical isolation-syndrome effects, even though emergence factors had been minimized.

Other studies have followed isolate behavior up to 5 years of age in a variety of situations. Early isolates remain deficient in exploratory behavior, motor activity, and positive social behavior, and continue to show excessive fear, withdrawal, and disturbance (for example, see Table 3). Both 6ME and 6ML isolates have developed high levels of aggression as juveniles and adults (Mitchell, Raymond, Ruppenthal, & Harlow, 1966), and have even directed physical attacks on neonates, a behavior rarely seen in mother or peer raised monkeys. Isolation effects, therefore, have persisted unaltered into adulthood even though the subjects have received extensive social and nonsocial experience after rearing.

Persistent Deficits in Pain Reactions

Response to noxious stimulation by five adult male 6-month isolates and five feral controls is currently being tested (Lichstein & Sackett, 1968). The monkey lives in a cage where all fluid is received from a tube mounted on one wall. Each subject is trained to touch the tube for 2 seconds, after which he receives a maximum of 8 seconds of water if he continues to touch the tube. Each time he breaks contact with the tube, or maintains contact for a full 10 seconds, he must reinitiate contact for more than 2 seconds before obtaining another drink. If the subject breaks tube contact before 2 seconds (partial contacts), no water is given. Every drink, therefore, must be preceded by a tube contact of at least 2 seconds, and the length of a drink is determined by how long contact is maintained after this period. When the subject is fully trained, a series of 21 increasing shock levels varying from about 10 microamps to 2.5 milliamps electrifies the drinking tube. A trial at a given shock level has two parts: (1) an initial shock period, during which the tube is electrified, and the monkey must overcome 2 seconds of shock in order to receive water; and (2) a safe period, during which the monkey can drink and reinitiate 2-second tube contacts without further shock. At each current level shock is on the tube only during partial contacts preceding and including the first full 2-second contact. The safe period ends, initiating the next shock level, when the monkey drinks for a full 8 seconds, or when 3 minutes elapse since the last tube contact in the safe period. Each subject was run in this fashion until he had either overcome every shock level or failed to make a tube contact within 24 hours. Two replications on each subject were conducted at 2-month intervals.

Three measures are presented in Table 5: (1) the number of partial tube approaches at the first five shock levels (currents less than 100 microamps), a measure of identifying differences in sensitivity to shock; (2) the shock value at which the subject refuses to make a contact

TABLE 5

Differences in Response to Electric Shock

PARTIAL CONTACTS AT CURRENT LESS THAN 100 MICROAMPS		
	ISOLATES	FERALS	
First Replication	13.2 (1.4–26.2)	1.9 (0.4–4.6)	$p = .016$
Second Replication	2.1 (.4– 5.6)	0.9 (0.0–2.8)	$p = .048$
TOLERATION LEVEL OF CURRENT		
	ISOLATES	FERALS	
First Replication	2.1 (.5–2.5)	1.4 (.9–2.0)	$p = .075$
Second Replication	2.5 (all 2.5)	1.4 (.8–2.3)	$p = .008$
PARTIAL CONTACTS DURING SAFE PERIODS		
	ISOLATES	FERALS	
First Replication	1.0 (0–2.3)	1.7 (.2–413)	$p = .210$
Second Replication	4.4 (.5–16.7)	2.3 (0–9.4)	$p = .028$

Note: Differences in response to electric shock by 5 adult males raised in total isolation during year 1, and by 5 feral control males. Data are presented for the average (1) partial contacts (escape-type responses) at very low current levels, (2) level of current at which the subject refuses to make further drinking tube contacts (maximum current = 2.5 milliamps), and (3) number of partial contacts during safe, no shock, periods after overcoming a given current level. Ranges are given in parentheses, along with Mann-Whitney U probabilities for group differences.

within 24 hours, a measure of shock toleration; and (3) the number of partial contacts during all safe periods, a measure of the generalized effects of shock.

Isolates averaged significantly more partial approaches at the low shock levels than did controls, suggesting that they were more sensitive to the effects of shock. Isolates generally tolerated higher levels of shock than did the controls. In the first replication four of the five isolates overcame the highest shock value, while in the second replication all isolates overcame the highest shock value. No feral control overcame the highest shock level in either replication. This suggests that isolates are less reactive to shock, or are unable or unwilling to inhibit approaches to the drinking tube even when faced with tissue-damaging current to the lips. Nonshock partial tube contacts, averaged over all safe periods, were not different in the first replication, but were higher in the second replication for the isolates. This suggests that after experiencing high shock levels in the first replication, isolates generalized shock effects to nonshock behavior. Water intake duration, averaged over all shock levels, revealed no significant differences between isolates ($X = 17.3$ seconds) and controls ($X = 14.8$ seconds) ($p > .30$), suggesting that thirst motivation factors did not affect the results.

These preliminary data suggest that abnormal responses to noxious stimulation have persisted into the adult behavior of isolates. This behavior presents an apparent anomaly in which the isolate has greater sensitivity to low current values, greater generalization of escape-type responses, but a higher tolerance for shock. This abnormal pain response appears to represent a qualitative difference in the sensory and perceptual systems underlying reception of, and reaction to, noxious input. Rearing in a variationless environment may thus produce a change in physiological mechanisms underlying pain reception, and apparently produces deficits in inhibitory behaviors relating to ability to stop responding in the face of pain.

Picture Isolation: Effects of Visual Stimulation on Development

In postrearing tests starting at 10 months of age the 9-month picture isolates (p. 23) were matched for age and sex with partial isolate controls (Pratt, 1967). For the next year these pairs received identical experiences. At 15 months, each matched set was paired with a peer-reared monkey of the same age and sex. A control group of 9-month total isolates, reared under identical procedures as picture isolates but without pictures, was studied under the same postrearing conditions.

In these studies care was taken to minimize emergence effects by gradually pacing exposure to novel and complex situations. These steps included (1) placing a wire front on the isolation cage, thus allowing the isolate to look out; (2) transport cage training at the isolation cage before taking the monkey to new environments; (3) 2 months of nonsocial adaptation to a novel test cage, (4) providing the first exposure to a real monkey by allowing each isolate to look at its matched partial isolate through a window for one week, then allowing one week of physical interaction, (5) 1 month of individual adaptation to a playroom, and (6) 2 months of paired experience in the playroom with the matched PI and peer-reared subject.

The results of this procedure were initially successful. When placed in a novel cage, isolates exhibited no more fear or withdrawal than PI controls, and had more environmental exploration. A novel test environment therefore did not produce emotional responses that inhibited exploration or lowered motor activity. These pacing procedures, nevertheless, did not eliminate isolation effects on social behavior.

From 18 to 21 months of age, all monkeys were tested in a playroom in triads of matched isolates, partial isolates, and peer-reared monkeys, and in quadrads containing pairs of animals in all combinations of the three groups. Figure 10 presents a profile of the average probability of occurrence for each class of behavior in the total behavioral repertoire of each group during the 3-month test period.

The two total isolate groups and the partial isolates were abnormal compared with the peer-reared controls. Socially elicited fear and nonsocial withdrawal and disturbance accounted for over 70% of total isolate behavior. Isolates had little nonsocial exploration, and no instances of positive social behaviors such as approach and play. Partial isolates also had high levels of disturbance and fear, but did perform nonsocial exploratory responses, and had low, but not zero, probabilities for positive social behaviors. Peer-raised monkeys had almost no fear or disturbance, were highest in nonsocial exploration and in positive social behaviors. Picture isolates differed from the 9-month total isolates in only one behavior, social fear ($p < .05$), indicating that picture rearing had no positive effects on social development, and may have produced some negative transfer.

These data reveal that viewing socially relevant stimuli during rearing

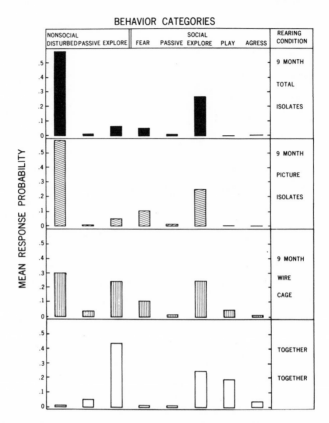

FIG. 10. Behavior profiles for three months of social tests in a playroom by animals reared for 9 months in total isolation, in total isolation with pictures of monkeys, in partial isolation, and together with peers in the same cage. The data are presented for nonsocial and social response categories that summarize the total repertoire of each group.

does not reduce isolation effects. The release of socially appropriate responses, such as fear with threat pictures and exploratory-play responses with infant pictures, fails to aid later social adjustment. Also, gradually pacing the introduction of novel and complex postrearing input fails to modify the typical isolate syndrome. Deficits similar to those seen following total isolation also appear in the behavior of partial isolates, who received visual and auditory, but not physical, stimulation from other animals during rearing. One hypothesis suggested by these facts is that isolation or partial isolation rearing retards the monkey's intellectual development, reflected in inability to acquire new responses or to inhibit or modify old responses. Data presented next relate to this issue.

Intellectual Development of Isolates

A series of experiments assessed the performance of isolates in the Wisconsin General Test Apparatus on object quality discrimination, learning set, and delayed response performance (Harlow, Schiltz, & Harlow, 1968). Isolation-reared subjects performed at least as well as feral, and other control groups, on these tests.

An example of learning set performance by five picture isolates and five partial-isolate controls, collected at 2.5 years of age, is shown in Figure 11. There are no differences in performance between these groups,

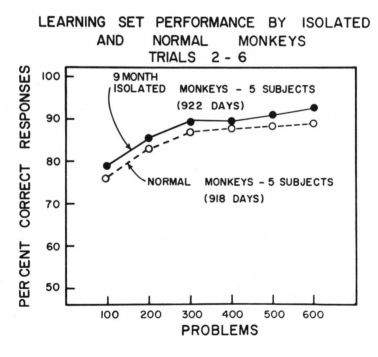

FIG. 11. Learning set performance on 6-trial object quality discrimination problems for picture isolates and partial isolate controls at 2.5 years of age.

and the data are representative for feral monkeys at this age. A major difference appeared between these groups, however, in adapting to the apparatus and test procedures before the actual start of discrimination training. Before learning tests can proceed, the animal must take food from a tray, push objects off foodwells into the tray, and continue to perform when screens are raised and lowered at the start and end of each trial. As shown in Table 6, picture isolates took much longer to adapt

TABLE 6

Time to Adaptation in WGTA Before Discrimination Training

GROUP	(1) Home-Cage Hand-Feeding	(2) Moving One-well Food Tray with Single Object Displacement	(3) Opaque Screen Lowered	(4) One-Way Screen Lowered	(5) Two-Well Food Tray
Picture Isolates	8.8	55.0	5.4	16.2	21.8
	(4–20)	(18–106)	(1–8)	(8–39)	(20–30)
Partial Isolates	5.2	20.2	4.8	5.2	8.2
	(5–6)	(17–30)	(4–5)	(2–6)	(5–20)
Probability	NS	.002	NS	.004	.016

Note: Means and ranges (in parentheses) for number of days to reach adaptation criteria in a WGTA prior to the start of discrimination training. Mann-Whitney U test probabilities are given for the significance of group differences at each adaptation stage.

than partial isolates, revealing a deficit in responding to novel objects and changes in experimental procedures. Yet once the isolate had spent over 3.5 months adapting to the situation, it performed at the same rate as other monkeys. Isolates did not have intellectual deficits on these tests, although they had large deficits in the ability or willingness to inhibit responses that competed with those demanded by the learning task.

A THEORY OF EARLY EXPERIENCE EFFECTS IN PRIMATES

An explanation of the effects reviewed in this paper is based on the following assumptions. Behaviorally, development involves adjustment to the demands of environmental stimulus changes and maturation-produced internal stimulus changes. Three primary mechanisms determine this process. The first involves reflexive and complex perceptual-motor systems based on genetic and prenatal factors. The second involves associative learning, built on unlearned processes, which lead to the acquisition and elaboration of perceptual, motor, and cognitive skills. This second mechanism determines development of new motor responses, transformation of previously performed responses into more complex patterns, and acquisition of perceptual responses that organize relations among stimuli. The third mechanism involves inhibitory processes that allow the individual to stop performing innate, emotional, or previously learned responses that have high probabilities of occurrence in its behavioral repertoire. The development of these inhibitory behaviors is a necessary condition for associative learning and response to change. Failure to inhibit responses that compete with attending to new stimuli and with performing new or modified responses functionally places the individual out of contact with the stimulus relationships, contiguities, or reinforcers necessary for the operation of the associative process.

The following hypotheses are offered within the context of these assumptions. (1) Persistent effects of rearing conditions on willingness or ability to modify behavior under conditions of stimulus change are a function of developing inhibitory behaviors early in life. Environments that do not produce gross physiological damage and that provide contingencies for inhibiting behavior will yield individuals that modify their behavior when presented with discrepancies between rearing and postrearing stimulation. Environments that do not afford such contingencies will yield individuals with permanent deficits in modifying behavior in response to discrepancy. A particularly important part of this process are rearing experiences that allow inhibition of emotional, self-oriented, or stereotyped responses when faced with uncertain, incongruous, intense, or noxious stimulation. (2) Associative conditioning, involving acquisition of specific motor and perceptual behaviors during rearing, is of secondary importance for behavioral development. If basic sensory-motor systems are intact, and if inhibitory behaviors are available, associative processes will function.

In this proposal, the major condition necessary for adequate postrearing behavior is the development during rearing of a nonspecific inhibitory response mode. In analogy, this mode represents the development of an information analyzing system that contains the following general concept: at times, it is necessary to inhibit ongoing or high probability responses in order to receive feedback from uncertain or changed environmental events concerning the meaning and information content, or the incentive and reinforcement potential, of the situation.

These views are similar to a neuro-behavioral model of emotion and motivation proposed by Pribram (1967). This model suggests that two neural inhibitory processes, involving "preparatory" and "participatory" mechanisms, organize the individual's behavior in the face of novelty or incongruity. The preparatory mechanism internally regulates neural organization by inhibiting sensory input, thereby preserving stable neural conditions. This preparatory mechanism often produces behaviors that are incompatible with the demands of a changed environment. The participatory mechanism inhibits processes that tend to maintain stable organization, allowing external input to modify neural patterns. This mechanism responds to input changes by incorporating information into ongoing neural organization, thus permanently increasing the complexity of the neural system. Pribram suggests that the adequacy of behavior in the face of change is determined by the balance of these two neural mechanisms, one inhibiting sensory input, the other operating on the basis of change. In terms of the present proposal, deficient rearing conditions are thought to produce individuals who filter out novel or complex input, operating primarily in the preparatory mode; while adequate rearing conditions produce individuals capable of inhibiting the preparatory process and acting on changed input.

Conditions for Inhibitory Development

Under normal ecological conditions, organism-environment interactions develop a continuous exchange in which behavior modifies the stimulus situation, and these effects on the environment feed back information that in turn modifies behavior. It is proposed that development of the inhibitory response mode in primates depends on experiencing variable feedback during attempts to control and manipulate social and nonsocial stimulation. Inhibitory behavior is thus assumed to develop out of the response variability that occurs whenever feedback from performance of unlearned or conditioned responses does not yield an expected outcome. Individuals reared with no response-contingent feedback or with completely unpredictable feedback will have little reason to vary their behaviors. Because response variability yields no useful information, it is expected that relatively stereotyped behaviors, stimulated more by internal than external conditions, will develop. Individuals reared under constant, perfectly predictable, response-contingent feedback should also develop a relatively invariant set of behaviors; but because these behaviors are partially controlled by external events, response variability under these conditions should be greater than that developed under unpredictable feedback. Maximum response variability should occur in situations involving partial, but not total, predictability about the effects contingent on responses. The specific effects of feedback might relate to several types of information concerning the perceptual attributes of stimuli (curiosity) or consequences relating to the individual's physical condition (tissue needs and pain) or "security" (e.g., contact comfort or the immediate state of a socially attached object). In general, these feedback effects concern the potential of the environment to provide either positive or negative incentives or reinforcers of unlearned or learned origin.

Given this analysis, it is hypothesized that the necessary conditions for developing the inhibitory response mode include rearing in environments that provide opportunities for controlling input, with at least some variability (relative uncertainty) in the feedback effects contingent on these controlling responses. It is also hypothesized that if experience in controlling the environment and receiving probabilistic feedback does not occur before the individual reaches a crucial maturational level, there will be permanent deficits in inhibitory abilities. Specifically, rearing conditions with the following characteristics will yield individuals differing in ability to inhibit competing responses when presented with discrepant input. In rank order from the least to greatest in producing inhibitory ability are environments (1) void of all varied input other than self-produced stimulation; (2) containing stimulus changes that are not contingent on the individual's responses; (3) containing response-contingent but totally unpredictable changes; (4) containing completely predictable response-contingent changes; and (5) containing an optimal balance between total predictability and total uncertainty concerning the effects of response-contingent changes. This final condition identifies the types of enriched environments that are expected to produce permanent increases in the ability of animals to respond appropriately to varied stimulation.

Reflexes, Emotionality, and Strain Differences

At least several factors will affect the development of inhibitory control. The presence and strength of neonatal reflexive behaviors will influence the temporal course of inhibitory development. In rhesus monkeys such reflexes include clasping, grasping, and clinging to almost any soft or rounded object, sucking, turning upright when placed on the back, upward climbing, and convulsive body jerking. Young infants cannot inhibit these responses when appropriate stimuli are presented. Generally, the only stimuli that will inhibit reflexes are those releasing other, more dominant, reflexes. This suggests that the onset of a crucial period for inhibitory development will occur when reflexive control wanes and nonreflexive responses increase in probability. In laboratory-born rhesus monkeys this occurs somewhere between the second and forth months (e.g., Mowbray & Cadell, 1962; Milbrath, 1968). This age may, of course, vary markedly between species, strains, and individuals.

A second set of factors concerns differences in "emotionality" produced by the interaction of genetic and prenatal variables (e.g., Henderson, 1967; Denenberg & Rosenberg, 1967). As hypothesized earlier, a major source of competing response tendencies lies in disturbance reactions elicited by discrepant, intense, or noxious input. It is clear that some species and strains are less reactive than others. In terms of this theory, such low emotional individuals are either genetically wired for, or prenatally develop, mechanisms that decrease the probability of withdrawal, disorientation, fear, hyperactivity, or immobility when faced with stimulus changes (e.g., Fuller, 1967). Low reactivity animals will, therefore, have a lower probability of performing incompatible, competing responses. For such individuals, early experience in learning to inhibit responses will be of limited importance. In essence, it is proposed that the principle behavioral characteristic of highly emotional individuals, differentiating them from those low in emotionality, is failure to inhibit unlearned or learned modes of responding that are incompatible with current stimulation. Postnatal treatments, such as handling and other stressors, that reduce later emotionality are thus assumed to derive their effect, at least in part, because they involve inhibition of reflexive and other high probability responses, and thereby produce development of the inhibitory response mode.

In terms of Pribram's neural model (1967), it might be assumed that at birth, emotional individuals operate primarily in the preparatory mode. Nonemotional individuals have already developed participatory neural structures, and therefore need little postnatal inhibition experience. Alternatively, high and low emotional individuals might develop equally in preparatory and participatory neural processes by birth. Due to a lack of discrepant stimulation early in life, however, participatory mechanisms may either fail to develop further or may atrophy in high emotional individuals, while in those low in emotionality changes in the participatory structures may be more resistant to "lack of use."

Evidence for the Inhibitory Response Proposal

Summary of Rearing Effects. The data on rearing condition effects in rhesus monkeys may be summarized as follows. (1) In addition to reflexes, these primates may possess complex, inborn, information processing and response mechanisms that normally underlie development of many social and nonsocial behaviors. The appearance and exercise of these unlearned behaviors early in life is not a sufficient condition for normal development. (2) Rearing in partial isolation, void of physical contact with mothers or peers but containing visual and auditory social stimulation, produces permanent deficits in social, emotional, maternal, sexual, and exploratory behaviors, although intellectual ability seems normal. (3) Rearing in total isolation in an unchanging perceptual world produces severe deficits in all areas of behavior except intellectual performance. These deficits occur even with adaptation to postrearing test situations during the rearing period, and after gradual pacing to novel, complex, and intense stimulus changes following rearing. Severe deficits also occur in monkeys raised in total isolation with varied visual pictorial input that is under completely predictable response-contingent control, and that elicits socially appropriate fear, play, and exploratory behaviors. These socially appropriate behaviors do not affect the stimulus pictures and therefore result in no relevant feedback to the animal concerning the effects of its behavior on the environment. (4) Two other important effects are permanent deficits in response to noxious input by isolates and hyperaggression following both inadequate mothering and isolation rearing.

Rearing Effects and Inhibition Theory

Pain. Adults reared in isolation appear to be more sensitive to low levels of shock than feral monkeys. Ferals, however, inhibit responding to an electrified drinking tube at lower shock levels than isolates, and ferals quickly inhibit escape-type responses during a safe period when the tube is not electrified. Isolates fail to inhibit tube contacts at extremely high current levels, and fail to inhibit escape-type responses during safe periods. Such effects are specifically predicted by the inhibition deficit theory.

General Isolation Effects. When living in early total or partial isolation, monkeys develop a response repertoire consisting mainly of self-directed behaviors such as clutching, rocking, huddling, mouthing, and biting, as well as stereotyped pacing and limb movements. Only low levels of outward-directed tactual and oral exploration of the inanimate environment occur in these situations. When isolation ends and new stimuli requiring outward-directed behaviors are presented, total and partial isolates continue to perform the behaviors developed during rearing, and fail to inhibit these responses even after years of social and nonsocial experience. In learning tests, however, isolates perform as well as other monkeys if they receive a protracted, gradual, adaptation schedule in the situation before actual learning problems are presented. During this adaptation period the animals eventually inhibit self-directed and stereotyped behaviors. It is interesting to note that successful adapation by isolates to a specific learning apparatus, with almost complete suppression of competing behaviors, and learning to physically contact other monkeys, fails to transfer to performance in any other social or nonsocial situation (Sackett, 1968). Most of these isolation effects appear to fit the inhibition failure model.

Aggression. It is possible that hyperaggression in motherless-mothered and isolation-reared monkeys develops from different causes. A common explanation, however, is available in the inhibition theory. High levels of threat and attack develop in laboratory-born rhesus monkeys between 2 and 3 years of age, especially in males, regardless of specific rearing conditions. In isolates, aggression is likely to be self-directed or directed toward inappropriate objects. The aggression of motherless-mothered animals often involves physical attack on other monkeys, while normally mothered individuals usually display aggression by threat postures, gestures, and vocalizations rather than physical violence. A major difference in rearing between these mothered groups lies in opportunity for inhibiting responses before the 6 to 7 months of life. Motherless-mothered offspring repeatedly approach and contact their mothers during the first 2 to 3 months, even though they are rejected and physically punished. This persistence in the face of punishment probably occurs because of the strong reflexive grasping and clinging behaviors present at these ages. During months 2 to 3 normally mothered animals are rarely rejected, but from months 4 to 6 they receive inhibitory opportunities when rejected by the mother during the normal separation process. Motherless-mothered offspring are less likely to receive this experience during months 4 to 6, when inhibitory behaviors are possible. In later peer interactions up to adulthood, the physical contact behaviors of inadequately mothered animals are more intense and more likely to involve biting, fur pulling, and bloodletting than the contact behaviors of feral-mothered monkeys. Because stimulation experienced after months 8 to 12 is identical for both types of mothered animals, it is suggested that inhibition of intense reactions such as aggression depends on feedback contingencies provided by the mother, or by peers, before months 8 to 12 of life. At these crucial ages isolates also do not have opportunities for learning response inhibition. Similar deficits in inhibitory control training may underlie the development of hyperaggression in these markedly different rearing conditions.

Other evidence for inhibitory failure in motherless-mothered offspring is seen in circus tests at 8 to 10 months of age involving preferences for the mother versus other adult females, and for adult females versus age-mates (Sackett, Griffin, Pratt, Joslyn, & Ruppenthal, 1967). Offspring of motherless and feral mothers prefer their own mother over strange females; but, inadequately mothered animals have a greater preference for their own mother than adequately mothered subjects. Offspring of feral mothers prefer an age-mate over an adult female, even though the adult female is the monkey's actual mother. Motherless-mothered subjects prefer the adult female, whether it is their own mother or a stranger. This suggests that feral-mothered monkeys can inhibit approach behavior toward familiar "attachment" stimuli, thereby exposing themselves to novelty; while motherless-mothered offspring fail to inhibit approach responses to familiar stimuli.

Peer rearing without mothers has generally produced behaviorally adequate animals. In this situation mutual contact, with two or more animals clinging to each other, occurs at high levels. This close physical contact provides variable feedback to each cage-mate. When a monkey in this situation attempts to play, eat, or locomote in space, another monkey is often clinging to its arm, leg, or body. In the normal course of moving about the cage the animal's responses are partially or totally inhibited by the responses of cage-mates. Such conditions should be adequate for the development of inhibitory responding and subsequent ability to adapt to new situations; a finding which is observed following peer rearing.

Critical Periods. The critical or sensitive period proposal receives support from several sources in addition to the analysis of motherless mothering already offered. Three months of total isolation from birth fails to drastically alter later adaptability, while 6 months of early isolation produces quantitative deficits in most response classes. This suggests that failure to receive inhibitory opportunities in the first 6 months, a sensitive period, results in permanent, quantitative, inhibitory response deficits. The finding that 9 to 12 months of total isolation permanently devastates almost every class of behavior, suggests that experience during this period is critical for the development of inhibitory behavior.

Comparative Evidence for the Inhibitory Response Proposal

At present, most of the evidence for this proposal is either indirect, or lies in post hoc explanation. Although the theory lends itself to empirical testing, few studies have been specifically and appropriately designed to manipulate opportunity for response control and variable feedback involving different sensory modalities at different maturational stages. The purposes of this paper (and space considerations) preclude a thorough review of comparative studies supporting the model, but several examples in different species are compatible with this theory.

Stimulus deficient rearing conditions have produced rats, dogs, chimpanzees, and physiologically normal, institution-reared, human children who are unable or unwilling to respond appropriately to environmental change. Deprivation rearing in rats yields hyperactivity or freezing behaviors in exploratory and learning situations that preclude systematic exploration of novel stimuli and compete with responses being conditioned (e.g., Woods, Fiske, & Ruckelshaus, 1961). Other studies varying input in specific modalities show that rats prefer familiar over novel, and perceptually simple over complex, stimuli in initial tests following rearing in perceptually simple environments (e.g., DeNelsky & Denenberg, 1967; Sackett, 1967a). In "reactive" dogs, deprivation rearing produces disoriented activity, hyperexploratory responses, and high levels of emotionality in postrearing situations (e.g., Fuller, 1967), and these anomalous behaviors lead to learning failures. In chimpanzees, stereotyped and repetitive locomotor and limb movements compete with responses needed to adjust to many postrearing situations (e.g., Davenport & Menzel, 1963). In institution-reared humans, lack of response-contingent input produces withdrawn, inactive children who score lower on tests of motor, language, social, and intellectual development than children who receive extra varied stimulation (e.g., Casler, 1965). Finally, inhibitory deficits have been postulated to underlie many learning changes and performance deficits in "normally reared" children at a critical age of 5 to 7 years (White, 1965).

REFERENCES

Arling, G. L., & Harlow, H. F. Effects of social deprivation on maternal behavior of rhesus monkeys. *Journal of Comparative and Physiological Psychology,* 1967, **64,** 371–377.

Casler, L. The effects of extra tactile stimulation on a group of institutionalized infants. *Genetic Psychology Monograph,* 1965, **71,** 131–175.

Clark, D. L. Immediate and delayed effects of early, intermediate, and late social isolation in the rhesus monkey. Unpublished doctoral dissertation, University of Wisconsin, 1968.

Cross, H. A., & Harlow, H. F. Prolonged and progressive effects of partial isolation on the behavior of macaque monkeys. *Journal of Experimental Research in Personality,* 1965, **1,** 57–64.

Davenport, R. K., & Menzel, E. W., Jr. Stereotyped behavior of the infant chimpanzee. *Archives of General Psychiatry,* 1963, **8,** 99–104.

DeNelsky, G. Y., & Denenberg, V. H. Infantile stimulation and adult exploratory behavior: Effects of handling upon tactual variation seeking. *Journal of Comparative and Physiological Psychology,* 1967, **63,** 309–312.

Denenberg, V. H., & Rosenberg, K. M. Nongenetic transmission of information. *Nature,* 1967, **216,** 549–550.

Fantz, R. L. The origin of form perception. *Scientific American,* 1961, **204,** 66–72.

Fox, M. W. Neuro-behavioral ontogeny: A synthesis of ethological and neurophysiological concepts. *Brain Research,* 1966, **2,** 3–20.

Fuller, J. L. Experiential deprivation and later behavior. *Science,* 1967, **158,** 1645–1652.

Griffin, G. A., & Harlow, H. F. Effects of three months of total social deprivation on social adjustment and learning in rhesus monkeys. *Child Development,* 1966, **37,** 534–547.

Gyllensten, L., Malmfors, T., & Norrlin, M. Growth alteration in the auditory cortex of visually deprived mice. *Journal of Comparative Neurology,* 1966, **126,** 463–469.

Harlow, H. F., & Harlow, M. K. Learning to love. *American Scientist,* 1966, **54,** 244–272.

Harlow, H. F., Harlow, M. K., & Hansen, E. W. The maternal affectional system of rhesus monkeys. In H. Rheingold (Ed.), *Maternal behavior in mammals.* New York: Wiley, 1963, Pp. 254–281.

Harlow, H. F., Joslyn, W. D., Senko, M. G., & Dopp, A. Behavioral aspects of reproduction in primates. *Journal of Animal Science,* 1966, **25,** 49–67.

Harlow, H. F. Schiltz, K. A., & Harlow, M. K. Effects of social isolation on the learning performance of rhesus monkeys. *Proceedings of the Second International Congress of Primatology,* in press.

Harlow, H. F., & Seay, B. Mothering in motherless mother monkeys. *British Journal of Social Psychiatry,* 1966, **1,** 63–69.

Hebb, D. O. The organization of behavior. New York: Wiley, 1949.

Henderson, N. D. Prior treatment effects on open field behavior of mice: A genetic analysis. *Animal Behavior,* 1967, **15,** 621–623.

King, J. A. Parameters relevant to determining the effect of early experience upon the adult behavior of animals. *Psychological Bulletin,* 1958, **55,** 46–58.

Lichstein, L., & Sackett, G. P. Unpublished data, 1968.

Melzack, R., & Scott, T. H. The effects of early experience on the response to pain. *Journal of Comparative and Physiological Psychology,* 1957, **50,** 155–161.

Milbrath, C. Developmental effects of early nonsocial enrichment in rhesus monkeys. Unpublished master's thesis, University of Wisconsin, 1968.

Mitchell, G. D., Raymond, E. J., Ruppenthal, G. C., & Harlow, H. F. Long-term effects of total social isolation upon the behavior of rhesus monkeys. *Psychological Reports,* 1966, **18,** 567–580.

Mitchell, G. D., Arling, G. L., & Møller, G. W. Long-term effects of maternal punishment on the behavior of monkeys. *Psychonomic Science,* 1967, **8,** 209–210.

Morgan, C. T., & King, R. A. *Introduction to Psychology,* 2nd ed., New York: McGraw-Hill, 1966.

Mowbray, J. B., & Cadell, T. E. Early behavior patterns in rhesus monkeys. *Journal of Comparative and Physiological Psychology,* 1962, **55,** 350–357.

Pratt, C. L. Social behavior of rhesus monkeys reared with varying degrees of early peer experience. Unpublished master's thesis, University of Wisconsin, 1967.

Pribram, K. H. Emotion: Steps toward a neurophysiological theory. In *Neurophysiology and Emotion,* New York: Rockefeller University Press, 1967.

Riesen, A. H. Effects of stimulus deprivation on the development and atrophy of the visual sensory system. *American Journal of Orthopsychiatry,* 1960, **30,** 23–36.

Rosenzweig, M. R. Environmental complexity, cerebral change, and behavior. *American Psychologist,* 1966, **21,** 321–332.

Rowland, G. L. The effects of total social isolation upon learning and social behavior in rhesus monkeys. Unpublished doctoral dissertation, University of Wisconsin, 1964.

Sackett, G. P. Effects of rearing conditions upon the behavior of rhesus monkeys. *Child Development,* 1965a, **36,** 855–868.

Sackett, G. P. Manipulatory behavior in monkeys reared under different levels of early stimulus variation. *Perceptual and Motor Skills,* 1965b, **20,** 985–988.

Sackett, G. P. Monkeys reared in visual isolation with pictures as visual input: Evidence for an innate releasing mechanism. *Science,* 1966, **154,** 1468–1472.

Sackett, G. P. Response to stimulus novelty and complexity as a function of rats' early rearing experiences. *Journal of Comparative and Physiological Psychology,* 1967a, **63,** 369–375.

Sackett, G. P. Some persistent effects of different rearing conditions on preadult social behavior of monkeys. *Journal of Comparative and Physiological Psychology,* 1967b, **64,** 363–365.

Sackett, G. P. Abnormal behavior in laboratory-reared rhesus monkeys. In M. W. Fox (Ed.), *Abnormal behavior in animals.* New York: Saunders, 1968a, chap. 18.

Sackett, G. P. The persistence of abnormal behavior following isolation rearing. In *The role of learning in psychotherapy.* London: CIBA, in press, 1968b.

Sackett, G. P., Porter, M., & Holmes, H. Choice behavior in rhesus monkeys: Effect of stimulation during the first month of life. *Science,* 1965, **147,** 304–306.

Sackett, G. P., Griffin, G. A., Pratt, C. L., Joslyn, W. D., & Ruppenthal, G. C. Mother-infant and adult female choice behavior in rhesus monkeys after various rearing experiences. *Journal of Comparative and Physiological Psychology,* 1967, **63,** 376–381.

Sackett, G. P., & Tripp, R. Unpublished data reported in part by G. P. Sackett, Innate mechanisms in primate behavior: Identification and casual significance. Paper presented at U.S.—Japan Seminar on Regulatory Mechanisms in behavioral development. Emory University, Atlanta, July 1968.

Sackett, G. P., Suomi, S. J., & Grady, S. Unpublished data reported in part by G. P. Sackett, Innate mechanisms, differential rearing experiences, and the development of social attachments in rhesus monkeys, at symposium on Attachment Formation, American Psychological Association, San Francisco, September 1968.

Scudder, C. L., Karczmar, A. G., & Lockett, L. Behavioral developmental studies on four genera and several strains of mice. *Animal Behavior,* 1967, **15,** 353–363.

Suomi, S. J. Master's thesis research, in preparation, University of Wisconsin, 1968.

Thorpe, W. H. *Learning and instinct in animals.* Cambridge: Harvard University Press, 1963.

Woods, P. J., Fiske, A. S., & Ruckelshaus, S. I. The effects of drives conflicting with exploration on the problem solving behavior of rats reared in free and restricted environments. *Journal of Comparative and Physiological Psychology,* 1961, **54,** 167–169.

White, S. H. Evidence for a hierarchical arrangement of learning processes. In L. P. Lipsitt & C. C. Spicker (Eds.), *Advances in child behavior and development,* vol. 2. New York: Academic Press, 1965.

Comments on Sackett's "Innate Mechanisms, Rearing Conditions, and a Theory of Early Experience Effects in Primates"

GILBERT W. MEIER
George Peabody College

THE FAILURE of isolation-reared animals to respond effectively under subsequent examination has been explained in a variety of ways: by differences in motivational factors, by the development of inappropriate body postures, by a limited intellectual development, by the conflict of hyperarousal states, by the failure to develop the response repertoire requisite for the testing, or by the intrusion of competing responses. Dr. Sackett has added another possibility to this list: the animal reared in isolation (the rhesus macaque, in this instance) experiences a paucity of environmental feedback and thereby fails to develop the inhibition mode of responding necessary for rapid adaptation to the later testing situation. In spite of the deficiency, however, that animal will learn discriminations and other complex responses as readily as the socially-reared control after extended provision is made for adaptation to the testing situation and procedure and his learning, in essence, the "rules of the game."

In support of his view, Dr. Sackett has offered an impressive array of corroborating data, primarily from studies undertaken at Wisconsin primate laboratories. In this regard, alone, he has provided a distinct service to the interested scientific community by bringing to public aware-

ness—with full identification and recognition—studies previously alluded
to but not cited. Since Dr. Sackett has contributed so significantly to
these research endeavors, his review of the major findings together with
the speculations on causal mechanisms are particularly noteworthy. One
must recognize, however, that the data as gathered from other primate
laboratories are not entirely supportive. Whether rearing in isolation
effects a significant long-lasting change in reproductive behaviors in
rhesus macaques and other nonhuman primates is not yet a matter of
widespread agreement (Meier, 1965; Missakian, in press; Rogers &
Davenport, in press). Whether this same rearing experience leaves un-
scathed multiple-problem and delayed-response learning is also open to
question (Davenport & Rogers, 1968; Davenport, Rogers, & Menzel, in
press). Although the wealth of data on these problems provided by the
Wisconsin group is impressive, one cannot help but look to other laboratories for corroboration and/or revelation of new and more subtle relations.

The reiteration of the value of cross-species comparisons based on
maturational ages, rather than time since conception, delivery, or weaning, is both reassuring and timely. The stress placed on the fundamental
character of the built-in response repertoire for traditional learning,
especially for the progressive learning process that is a part of behavioral
development, is a significant move to correct a long-standing deficiency
of orientation. In a broad conceptual analysis as is proposed here, however, Dr. Sackett naturally raises many issues, and in his attempts at
resolutions begs questions of interpretation and balance. Some would
wonder, for example, whether the view that genetic factors provide limits
on organismic development adequately reflects recent research and behavioral theory. Current thought emphasizes the continuing interaction
between the organism at all ages and its immediate environment. Also
emphasized is that bases may be genetically provided, but the limits of
individual adjustment are described by the organism-environment interaction. In the context of the studies reviewed here, one must recall that
the behavior of the isolate, laboratory-reared monkey is still distinctly
simian, while being unique in that the repertoire may only overlap briefly
that of the feral-reared animal. Others would be dismayed with the relatively short shift—one sentence only—given to prenatal factors in Dr.
Sackett's enumeration. Although time and space limitations may have
precluded a lengthy discussion of prenatal and genetic factors as distinct
from the postnatal factors that occupy the central orientation of Dr.

Sackett's review, one would wish to learn of examples of these factors and how in any fundamental way they differ from those postnatal factors discussed much more fully. Further, does the organism, under the conditions relevant to the studies discussed, really acquire new responses or does it make old responses under new stimulus conditions or under new reinforcement contingencies? Or is the in-cage behavior of the isolate-reared monkey indistinguishable from that of the feral-reared youngster? The peculiar stereotypes of the former, even in its own home situation, belie Dr. Sackett's contention.

Overall, these are comparatively minor reservations. More important, to the view of this critic, are questions regarding the positive features of the rearing experiences of the isolated infant and the temporal characteristics of early learning, broadly conceived. Both deal with the behavioral content of the rearing period.

Dr. Sackett fails to recognize here the possibility and form of response acquisition by the isolate-reared monkeys during the rearing period. Given the barren ecology in which these monkeys passed their infancies, the later appearance of self-directed behavior is not only understandable, but expected. The particular pattern of behavior is determined by the evocation by even this impoverished environment of certain built-in responses and by the occurrence of certain reinforcement contingencies, admittedly limited in variety, such as those of the clasping of furry body parts or of self-erotic stimulation. In all of these comparisons of the behaviors of wild-reared and laboratory-reared animals, one must remember that the behaviors of the latter group are not abnormal in any meaningful sense. The rearing conditions are. Given its particular rearing experiences and its phylogenetic history, the isolate-reared animal behaves predictably and in a manner that cannot be considered pathologic (cf. Mason, Davenport, & Menzel, 1968).

In the entirely novel stimulus complex of the testing situation, all animals respond as though to reduce the magnitude of the discrepancy with environments previously experienced. The magnitude of this discrepancy, however, is much greater for the isolation-reared monkeys than for the mother- or feral-reared animals and always in the direction of greater variety in the testing than in the rearing situation. Both the severity and duration of the withdrawal response—the responses that reduce the discrepancy of this magnitude and sign—are, therefore, prolonged. When withdrawal behaviors diminish and a stage of approach-adaptation behavior is reached, both the isolate- and social-reared animals respond in ways typical of their behaviors in their particular home environments. The typical testing situation is such that the exploratory behaviors—the responses made to discrepant situations of small magnitude—of the social-reared animal are immediately reinforced. Such behaviors yielding environmental manipulation have not been developed so fully in the isolate-reared animals because of the absence of varied stimulation and of such regularities of environmental change—reinforcement—as categorized by Dr. Sackett. Consequently, behaviors of these animals appear grossly inappropriate, as well they should, through their failure to inhibit certain responses to "new" or "strange" stimuli and the failure to establish adequate approach behaviors leading to environmental manipulation. This monkey's problem is not only the paucity of learning experiences, particularly those pertaining to stimulus differentiation, but more importantly the occurrence of inappropriate learned stimulus-response contingencies.

My second point concerns the temporal factors of behavioral maturation and of the experimental design as it pertains to the rearing procedure. For example, during the first two months following birth, the rhesus monkey infant shows a generalized pattern of approach behavior that is slowly but incompletely replaced by withdrawal behaviors especially noticeable in a complex social rearing situation. Under those conditions of interactions with other animals, the infant of about six months of age grimaces, vocalizes, and rapidly flees sudden confrontation by an adult other than its mother. Otherwise, it displays distinct hesitance in its approach to other animals in the social group. Aspects of these behaviors have been reported for infants reared with their mothers in paired isolation; some, even, are shown by animals stimulated only by pictures of aggressing monkeys, as Dr. Sackett has described. Not to be minimized in this context of infant-adult interaction is the changing pattern of behaviors of the adult to the rapidly-maturing infant. In a group social situation, the initial fear and withdrawal, then the masterful tolerance, and subsequently the comical fatherly indulgence by the adult male rhesus is instructive. Both the behaviors of the infant and the adult have a built-in character, presumably elicited by the features of the display and behavior of the other while being resistant to the influence of experience offered by previous similar encounters. In brief, although not vigorously researched, this maturational pattern of approach and withdrawal behavior is a species characteristic, reminiscent of maturational patterns in certain avian and less complex mammalian species.

For this discussion of early experience effects in primates, the maturational pattern of these two classes of behaviors—approach and withdrawal—is especially significant. Seemingly, the initial behaviors in a reasonably constant environment are those of approach to new stimuli. Only as the animal's manipulative and locomotor capabilities improve, do fear displays and withdrawal behaviors develop. In a social situation these responses are reinforced and the approach responses are selectively extinguished and become appropriately inhibited to others than the mother, age-peer, and young siblings. In a situation of social isolation at this age, the reinforcement contingencies are limited and not functionally related to the enhancement of one class of behaviors (withdrawal) while diminishing the generalized, undifferentiated appearance of the other (approach). Those contingencies that do exist erratically enhance and/or diminish both classes. Later, when confronted with the usual discrimination learning situation, the isolate-reared animal displays not only the behaviors he has learned during his rearing experience but his failure to inhibit those that the social-reared monkey inhibited "as a matter of course." Any long range modification of the behaviors of isolate-reared animals must include both features: the competing and the irrelevant responses.

In sum, I believe Dr. Sackett should be applauded for his efforts in bringing the built-in response system of the infant into the conceptual foreground and for offering a bridge in theory between aspects of behavioral development and of behavioral modification typified multiple-problem learning. I, for one, find the notion of "response inhibition mode," a construct suggestive of traits and other simplistic, all-encompassing individual characterizations, difficult to accept. At this time, I find the data base for such a concept unconvincing—sometimes even conflicting—and the heuristic value for future research, moot. I am confident, however, that Dr. Sackett will attack these questions of reasonableness with careful experimentation, and will return to us with specific data by which his concepts can be more properly judged.

REFERENCES

Davenport, R. K. and Rogers, C. M. Intellectual performance of differentially reared chimpanzees: I. Delayed responses. *American Journal of Mental Deficiency,* 1968, **72,** 674–680.

Davenport, R. K., Rogers, C. M., and Menzel, E. W., Jr. Intellectual performance of differentially reared chimpanzees: II. Discrimination-learning set. *American Journal of Mental Deficiency,* (In press).

Mason, W. A., Davenport, R. K., Jr., and Menzel, E. W., Jr. Early experience and the social development of rhesus monkeys and chimpanzees. In G. Newton and S. Levine (Eds.), *Early experience and behavior.* Springfield, Ill.: C. C. Thomas, 1968. Pp. 440–480.

Meier, G. W. Other data on the effects of social isolation during rearing upon adult reproductive behaviour in the rhesus monkey (*Macaca mulatta*). *Animal Behaviour,* 1965, **13,** 228–231.

Missakian, E. A. Reproductive behavior of socially deprived male rhesus monkeys (*Macaca mulatta*). In C. R. Carpenter (Ed.), *Proceedings, Second International Congress of Primatology.* Basel: Karger (In press).

Rogers, C. M. and Davenport, R. Sexual behavior of differentially reared chimpanzees. In C. R. Carpenter (Ed.), *Proceedings, Second International Congress of Primatology.* Basel: Karger (In press).

Experimental Programming of Life Histories and the Creation of Individual Differences: A Review[1]

Victor H. Denenberg
Purdue University

PERHAPS THE MOST difficult and baffling problem in behavioral science today is that of trying to understand why an adult organism acts the way it does. Why are some animals aggressive while others are passive? Why are some curious and interested in novel events, even to the point of exploring something "because it is there"? And why is it that some animals appear capable of coping with massive environmental inputs of a complex informational nature without any breakdown in their integrity while others become upset when there is a relatively minor change in their environmental structure?

Partial answers come to mind immediately. Genetic factors are obviously relevant. The organism's early experiences clearly have impact upon his subsequent performance. The cultural milieu in which one grows up helps shape an animal's behavior. The stimulus events at the moment are, of course, immediately important. For those who view all organisms within a broad biological framework, the evolutionary history of a species (especially behavioral evolution) is also critically important.

One could expand upon this list but I think the point is clearly made:

1. Much of the author's research described by this paper was supported by Program Project Grant Number HD-02068 from the National Institute of Child Health and Human Development.

the behavior of any organism is a complex function of biological, ecological, physical, psychological, and cultural inputs. Knowledge from
any one discipline, no matter how complete, will not be sufficient to
account for the behavior of an adult animal. It is apparent that, ulti-
mately, a multidisciplinary attack will have to be made on this problem.
Before one can run, however, it is necessary that one know how to
walk. And before an interdisciplinary attack on this problem can be
made, it is necessary that there be systematic information within each
discipline concerning how its particular variables act to affect adult behavior patterns. We have made a modest start in this direction through
our research involving experimental programming of life histories in the
rat.

EXPERIMENTAL PROGRAMMING OF LIFE HISTORIES

Since I am an experimental psychologist interested in early experiences, I choose to ask the question: How do different experiences over
time combine to affect adult behavior? One of our basic assumptions is
that an organism's behavior at any moment in time is determined, to a
significant extent, by his accumulated past experiences. Often it is not
one isolated experience in an animal's background that is the critical
determiner of his action, but a particular combination of experiences. It
also seems reasonable to assume that all past experiences will not have
equal impact. Some will tend to cancel each other out, others will
summate together, while still others will interact in a complex fashion.
Some of the animal's experiences may affect him only during a relatively
brief period of his life-span and not leave any residue that has long-term
effects. Other combinations of experiences may cause behavioral and
physiological modifications throughout the complete life of the animal
and may, indeed, significantly determine the length of the life-span. In
fact, some of these combinations of experiences may have such a broad
impact that the behavior and physiology of subsequent generations are
significantly modified.

The manner in which different experiences, singly and in combination
with other experiences, affect a particular adult behavior pattern is not
well known. Research in the field of infantile stimulation and early
experience has isolated a number of procedures that have been shown to
affect a wide variety of behavioral and physiological responses, but most
studies to date have not investigated the effects of combining different

experiences. The usual procedure has been to vary the organism's experience during one phase of his developmental history (between birth and weaning for infantile stimulation, from weaning up to early adulthood for much of the early experience work), keeping everything else constant, and then testing the animals in adulthood to assess the effects of earlier stimulation.

Like other researchers, my colleagues and I started out in this manner of varying one experimental condition at a time during early development and studying its consequences in adulthood. Recently, though we have begun to combine various experiences in a spatial and temporal framework that allows us to program different life-history patterns by generating different schedules of experience for our animals. In essence we take a large group of homogeneous animals, expose them to different programs of life-history experiences throughout their lifetime, and then find that the various subgroups (defined by the schedule of experience that each has received) are now heterogeneous. In other words, we find marked behavioral differences among our experimental groups on a variety of tests. When one talks about an animal's behavior pattern varying as a function of his schedule of experience, then one is talking about experimentally produced individual differences or "personalities." I feel that one of the values of early experience research is in allowing us to create, by experimental manipulations, different types of personalities. I will develop this theme more fully later in this report.

CONCEPTUAL FRAMEWORK

Having decided that our approach will be that of varying experiences over time, how does one place this into a conceptual framework and from there set up appropriate experimental operations? Our conceptual framework is relatively simple. We believe that in order to understand an organism's behavior, it is necessary to have information concerning that organism's experience at least from the time of birth. It is even more preferable if one has information concerning the nature of the mother of the experimental animal.

Having decided the point in time when one should initiate experimental manipulations, the next conceptual question concerns the nature of the experimental manipulations. Two broad classes of events appeared to us to be very critical in influencing and shaping an animal's future behavior: social interactions and stress experiences. Social interactions are obviously necessary for the development of all mammalian organisms, and the importance of stress experiences during development has been shown in a variety of research contexts. It is also apparent that these two classes are not necessarily independent of each other.

This is a sufficient conceptual framework to allow us to think about experimental operations. We wished to manipulate independent variables that could be conceptualized as falling within the class of events called social interactions or stress experiences and that could be administered to animals during their early life.

At this point it seemed most reasonable to select independent variables that had been empirically verified by our previous research. But before doing this, we had one more conceptual barrier to face. There are many different experimental operations that meet the criteria set forth above and that could have been chosen for experimental manipulations. Which of these should be picked? The criterion we applied was that the experimental operations that we chose for manipulation should all have impact upon the same behavioral process in adulthood. Since much of our previous research in infantile stimulation had shown that we were affecting the behavioral construct of "emotional reactivity" in adulthood, we decided to select experimental variables that were known to affect this particular behavioral dimension. More specifically, we chose variables that were known to modify open-field activity and defecation—which have been our primary measures of the construct of emotional reactivity (Denenberg, 1969b).

EXPERIMENTAL OPERATIONS

Within the framework described we selected four experimental variables for manipulation. Two of these variables involve the technique called "handling." The maternity cages in which our pregnant rats are kept are inspected once a day. Whenever a litter is found, the tray is removed from the maternity cage with the young on it, the mother remaining in the cage. Litters are sexed at this time and are reduced to eight young (depending upon the requirements of the experiment, the litters may have as many males as possible, as many females as possible, or any combination of male and female). The nonhandled controls are then returned to their maternity cage and are not disturbed again until weaning at 21 days. The shavings are not changed at any time during the nursing period, and food and water are available through external means.

The handled animals, on the other hand, are placed singly into one gallon tin cans containing shavings. They are left in the cans for three minutes and are then returned to the maternity cage. This procedure of placing animals singly into cans for three minutes and then returning them to the maternity cage is what we call "handling." This procedure is generally repeated once a day from Day 1 of life through Day 20, but the number of days of handling and the particular dates of handling may vary from one experiment to another.

In terms of the conceptual criteria set forth above, handling is a form of stress experience (Denenberg, 1964; Denenberg, Brumaghim, Haltmeyer, & Zarrow, 1967). In addition, handling probably affects social interactions since the pups are removed from the cage and then returned, which means that the mother is involved in retrieving the pups, packing them together into the nest, hovering over them, etc.

The four independent variables that we chose for programming life experiences and their effects upon open-field performance are as follows.

Handling in infancy. Many studies from different laboratories have shown that rats which are handled daily between birth and weaning are much more active and defecate less in the open field than do nonhandled controls (see Denenberg, 1964, 1967, 1969a for reviews).

Handling of mothers of experimental subjects. Since handling acts to reduce emotional reactivity, a natural question was to ask, for our female subjects, whether the handling experience that they had received in their infancy would have any effect upon their offspring. What we expected to find was that females which had been handled in infancy would have less emotional offspring because they would somehow communicate to their offspring nonemotional behavior. In fact, we already had data showing that offspring emotionality was related to maternal emotionality through both genetic and nongenetic mechanisms (Denenberg, Ottinger, & Stephens, 1962; Ottinger, Denenberg, & Stephens, 1963). We did indeed get effects, but they were in a direction opposite to expectations (Denenberg & Whimbey, 1963). We found that offspring of handled females were less active in the open field than were offspring of nonhandled females.

Preweaning rearing habitat. Typically, pregnant laboratory rats are placed into a maternity cage where they give birth and rear their young. There is nothing sacrosanct about this environment, and there is certainly no evidence that this is the optimal setting in which to raise one's offspring. In fact, one can develop a good rationale for putting the pregnant mother into a larger and more complex environment (this comes closer to approximating the rat's natural ecology), and so we did a study in which pregnant rats were placed into Hebb-type enriched free environments where they gave birth to and reared their young until weaning (Morton, 1962). We found that rats that have been reared in this habitat until weaning were more active in the open field than were control animals raised in maternity cages.

Postweaning habitat. At the time of weaning, laboratory rats are usually placed into small cages where they remain until called forth by a researcher to engage in some behavior that the experimenter finds interesting. From the human point of view life in such a small cage appears to be exceedingly monotonous and may act to increase an animal's emotional reactivity by restricting his behavioral degree of freedom. It would appear reasonable to assume that an animal raised in

TABLE 1

Experimental Design for Programming Life Histories

CONCEPTION TO DAY 21 EXPERIENCE OF NATURAL MOTHERS IN THEIR INFANCY	DAYS 1–20 HANDLING EXPERIENCE OF PUPS	DAYS 1–21 PRE-WEANING HOUSING	DAYS 21–42 POST-WEANING HOUSING
NH	NH	MC	LC
NH	NH	MC	FE
NH	NH	FE	LC
NH	NH	FE	FE
NH	H	MC	LC
NH	H	MC	FE
NH	H	FE	LC
NH	H	FE	FE
H	NH	MC	LC
H	NH	MC	FE
H	NH	FE	LC
H	NH	FE	FE
H	H	MC	LC
H	H	MC	FE
H	H	FE	LC
H	H	FE	FE

NH = nonhandled controls, H = handled, MC = maternity cage, FE = free environment, LC = laboratory cage a more complex environment after weaning would display different types of behavior in an open-field test situation than would cage-reared animals. This assumption was tested in two experiments, and in each instance the rats reared in free environments after weaning were found to be more active in the open field than were cage-reared controls (Denenberg & Morton, 1962, 1964).

Each of these four variables had been shown to affect open-field behavior when manipulated singly. What would happen to the animal's behavior when these variables were combined? We decided to test each variable at two levels as follows:

Mother of experimental subjects: handled or not handled in her infancy.

Experience of experimental subjects: handled or not handled in infancy.

Preweaning habitat: maternity cage or free environment until weaning (21 days).

Postweaning habitat: laboratory cage or free environment experience from weaning until 42 days of age.

The complete combination of these variables gives us a 2^4 factorial design with 16 different programs of experience for our animals. The experimental design is shown in Table 1.

EXPERIMENTALLY CREATED INDIVIDUAL DIFFERENCES

The experimental design presented in Table 1 is a 2 x 2 x 2 x 2 factorial, and anyone who has had courses in statistics knows that such a design is evaluated by means of the analysis of variance procedure. There is, however, another and very different way of looking at that experimental design—namely, through the eyes of a psychometrician.

In the usual analysis of variance approach to the design in Table 1, a number of animals would be randomly assigned to each of the 16 treatment combinations. These would be animals from different litters so that genetic differences in the population from which one was sampling would be randomly distributed among the 16 treatments. After computing the analysis of variance for any particular criterion measure, if the researcher found significant main effects and interactions, he would attribute the significant findings to the independent variables that he had manipulated in his experiment. He would be most unlikely to conclude that the differences were caused by genetic factors or other uncontrolled variables among the 16 groups since, if he were a competent researcher, he employed randomization. Of course, the experimenter recognizes that he would be wrong 1% or 5% of the time, depending upon his criterion for rejecting the null hypothesis, and he is willing to accept that risk. Beyond the usual sampling errors in any experiment, the differences among the 16 groups depicted in Table 1 are free of genetic variance. This is a very important consideration, and I will return to it again in a moment.

Why should the groups in Table 1 differ? The answer, obviously, is that they would differ as a function of the independent variables that had been introduced into the experiment. If no independent variables had been manipulated, one would expect to obtain differences among the 16 random groups no more frequently than chance would allow. In other words, within sampling error, the 16 groups would be homogeneous if they were all treated the same way throughout the experiment.

Let's make a conceptual shift: think of each of the 16 means in Table 1 as an "ideal individual." These are ideal individuals in two senses: (1) the difference among these 16 individuals (i.e., the 16 group means) cannot be attributed to genetic differences, and (2) the differences are attributable to their experimental histories. We start our experiment, therefore, with 16 homogeneous individuals and any difference that we find among these individuals must be a function of their programmed life-history experiences. We may thus conceive of the design in Table 1 as an experimental method for creating individual differences independent of genetic background. This may be thought of as the first step toward an experimental science of individual differences (Denenberg & Whimbey, 1968). In other words, the group difference model of the experimental psychologist is translated into the individual difference model of the psychometrician via the design in Table 1.

The analytical procedures used by the psychometrician to evaluate individual differences are, of course, quite different from the analytical procedures used by the experimental psychologist to evaluate group differences. The psychometrician uses correlational techniques while the experimental psychologist uses analysis of variance procedures. Since the experiment in Table 1 was conceived within the individual difference framework, it follows that one should use the methodology of the psychometrician. We decided to give the animals in the experiment a battery of tests, obtain the intercorrelations among these test scores, and then factor analyze the results. The object of all this, of course, was to see whether a meaningful set of individual difference dimensions could be created by our experimental manipulations. If so, this would give substance to our belief that one could engage in an experimental science of individual differences by programming life histories. If not, this would suggest that the genetic variance is so overriding that it is not possible to talk about individual differences independent of genetics (Whimbey & Denenberg, 1966, 1967).

As in any correlational study, a decision had to be made with respect to the nature of the test battery to be employed. For this study the decision was based both upon theoretical considerations as well as empirical information. I had hypothesized that one of the major effects of infantile stimulation was to modify emotionality. The formal statement is that "emotional reactivity is reduced as a monotonic function of amount of stimulus input in infancy" (Denenberg, 1964, p. 138). Supporting this argument were research findings from a number of experimenters who had manipulated the early experiences of their animals and who had measured emotional reactivity in adulthood. The various measures included activity and defecation in the open field (Denenberg & Smith, 1963; Denenberg & Whimbey, 1963), consummatory behavior following stress of water deprivation (Levine, 1957, Spence & Maher, 1962) and electric shock (Levine, 1958), defecation and activity during habituation to an avoidance conditioning apparatus (Levine, 1956), and judgments of timidity (Hunt & Otis, 1963). An implicit assumption in this theory is that these various operational measures are all sampling the same construct of emotional reactivity. No one had tested this assumption, however, and so a number of tests, all of which were presumed to measure emotional reactivity, were included in the battery. If there were such a construct as emotional reactivity, then one would expect to find the tests clustered in one factor of the factor analysis.

And this raises another problem: a difficulty with the construct of emotional reactivity is that one of the common methods of measuring it is by means of the locomotor activity of an animal. Locomotion, however, has also been used to measure the behavioral dimension of curiosity or exploratory behavior. Perhaps emotionality and exploratory behavior are bipolar parts of the same dimension, or perhaps they are two independent dimensions. In either case, it seemed important to try to separate these two dimensions, if indeed they were separable. Toward this end, several tests of exploratory behavior were also included in the test battery.

Finally, we chose several other dependent variables to place into the battery because these variables had been found by previous research to be sensitive (i.e., to discriminate significantly) to the particular early experience variables that we were using in this design. In addition, by seeing where these particular variables entered into the factor loadings, it would help in understanding the meaning of the factor loadings. These variables included avoidance learning, social preference, and body weight.

The Test Battery

Table 2 summarizes the tests applied, the measure obtained, and the age of testing. It will be convenient to refer to this table as each test is described.

TABLE 2

Testing Schedule and Test Variable Number

(From Whimbey and Denenberg, 1967a)

AGE	TEST	VARIABLE	VARIABLE #
220	Emotional rating	Rating	39
220–223	Open field	Activity[a]	40, 41, 42, 43, 20
		Defecation[a]	28, 29, 30, 31, 21
		Urination[a]	34, 35, 36, 37, 38
		Latency[a]	1, 2, 3, 4, 33
		Center squares totaled over 4 days	32
224	Novel stimuli box	Time in stimuli half	7
		Number of crossings	5
225	Social stimulus box	Time in stimulus half	8
		Number of crossings	6
226–230	Avoidance learning and defecation	Number of avoidances[b]	22, 23, 24, 25, 26, 27
		Latency to cross barrier[b]	12, 13, 14, 15, 16
		Defecation during learning trials on Day 226	18
		Defecation during learning trials on Day 230	19
230	Body weight	Body weight	17
231–232	Activity wheel and consummatory behavior	Activity 8:30 A.M.— 12:30 P.M.	9
		Activity 12:30 P.M. —10:30 P.M.	10

AGE	TEST	VARIABLE	VARIABLE #
		Activity 10:30 P.M. —8:30 A.M.	11
		Food consumption 8:30 A.M.— 10:30 P.M.	44
		Food consumption 10:30 P.M.— 8:30 A.M.	45
		Water consumption 8:30 A.M.— 10:30 P.M.	46
		Water consumption 10:30 P.M.— 8:30 A.M.	47
233	Open-field	Activity	48
		Defecation	49
70–73[c]	Open-field	Total activity over the 4 days	50
74–78[c]	Avoidance learning	Total latency over 5 days of training	51

[a] The first four variable numbers refer to the scores obtained on Days 1–4. The fifth variable number is the sum over Days 1–4. Variable 33 of open-field latency is the sum of dichotomized scores rather than raw scores.

[b] The first five variable numbers refer to the scores obtained on Days 1–5. Variable 27 is the total number of avoidances over the 5 days. Variables 12–16 are the log of the total latencies on the respective days. The total latency over 5 days was not used.

[c] The animals used to obtain these variables were littermates of the subjects used in the present study.

Emotionality rating. When the experimenter first took the rat from the cage at 220 days of age he rated the animal on a two-point scale: (1) struggled and tried to escape; (2) did not try to escape.

Open-field. Immediately after the emotionality rating the rat was placed into an open field consisting of 25 9-inch squares. During the 3 minutes that the animal was in the field, the following data were recorded: total number of squares entered, total number of fecal boluses, presence or absence of urination, latency to leave the starting square, and number of center squares entered. Each animal was tested for 4 consecutive days in the field.

Novel stimuli box. The day after the termination of open-field testing each animal was placed into a 10-inch x 26-inch rectangular black wooden box. One half of the box was empty. A variety of novel stimuli, including a bell, pieces of metal, wire, wood, and rubber, were tied in the other half of the box. A child's pinwheel, which was turned by an airjet, was also present in this half of the box. The amount of time spent in the stimulus half of the box and the total number of crossings from one half to the other were recorded.

Social stimulus box. This apparatus was identical to the novel stimuli unit except that a tethered adult rat of the same sex was in the stimulus half of the box. The other half was again empty. The same measures were obtained here as with the novel stimuli test.

Avoidance learning and defecation. The animals next received 5 days of avoidance learning shuttlebox training. The reinforcer was .5 ma. of current with a CS of buzzer and light. Ten trials were given per day. The total number of avoidances per day and the average latency per day were recorded.

The total number of boluses deposited during the training sessions during the first day and the last day of learning were also recorded.

Body weight. After the last trial in the learning apparatus each animal was weighed.

Activity wheel and consummatory behavior. Total number of revolutions in an activity wheel were recorded for three time intervals during a 24-hour period. The amount of food and water consumed during the 14 hours that the lights were on and the ten hours that the lights were off was also recorded.

Open field. The final test for these particular animals took place on Day 233 when they were given a 3-minute open-field test and activity and defecation were recorded.

Open-field and avoidance learning measures on littermates. Littermates of the animals in this study had received the same experimental treatment and had been used in another experiment starting at 70 days of age. Between 70–73 days of age these littermates had been tested in the open field. The total activity score of the littermates summed over four days of testing was used in this analysis. From days 74–78 these littermates had also received avoidance learning training, and their total latency for the five days of training was also entered into this analysis.

Experimental Design and Results

The 16 experimental groups in Table 1, in combination with the variables of sex, result in 32 experimental groups. Three animals from different litters were randomly assigned to each group. In a few instances a male and a female from the same litter were used in the respective treatment combinations.

In order to have a significant correlation in the usual type of correlational analysis, it is necessary that there be significant differences among individuals. Analogously, in this design it is necessary that there be significant differences among the group means in order to obtain significant correlations. Analyses of variance of the first 49 variables listed in Table 2 found a large number of significant main effects and interactions, indicating that the experimental treatments had produced significant differences among the groups on the various measures. (See Whimbey, 1965, for detailed information on these analyses.)

Next, the scores for the three males and the three females within each of the 16 experimental groups were combined and averaged for each variable. These mean scores represent the performance of the ideal individuals. Intercorrelations were then obtained among 46 of the variables (Variables 20, 21, 27, 33, and 38 were eliminated from this analysis so as not to include both part scores and total scores) and were factor analysed. This factor analysis included nine factors (Whimbey & Denenberg, 1967a). The pattern of factor loadings indicated that the same variable obtained on the same apparatus on different days tended to measure the same thing. Because this redundancy tends to distort the factor structure, it is necessary to have a more proportional representation of a variable in order to identify common factors. Twenty-three variables were selected from the original group and these were factor analyzed anew. Six factors were orthogonally rotated. The rotated factor loadings are presented in Table 3 where the variable numbers are the same as in Table 2.

Factor 1 is labeled "emotional reactivity." Defecation over four days of open-field testing (V. 21), defecation in the open field on test Day 14 (V. 49), defecation on the avoidance learning apparatus on Day 5 (V. 19), and ratings of emotionality (V. 39) all have positive loadings. Food and water consumed during the day (Vs. 44, 46) have negative loadings as do the variables of number of crossings and time in the stimulus half of the novelty box (Vs. 5, 7). It had been expected that the novel stimuli box would induce "curiosity," but observations of the rat's behavior indicated that the noise from the air hose and the pinwheel caused many of the animals to run away and freeze rather than explore. The novelty box thus made the animals "fearful" rather than curious.

TABLE 3

Loadings of the 23 Variables (Including Total Open-Field Activity at
70 and 220 Days of Age) on 6 Orthogonal Factors[a]
(From Whimbey and Denenberg, 1967a)

	FACTORS					
VARIABLES	1	2	3	4	5	6
5	—.418	.276	—.371	.057	—.636	.229
6	—.228	.324	—.201	—.132	—.777	.186
7	—.529	—.060	—.435	.431	—.188	—.046
8	—.051	.033	—.115	—.059	.234	—.819
10	.096	.253	—.341	.315	—.044	.787
11	.067	.573	—.675	.191	—.020	.194
12	—.037	—.233	—.940	—.007	—.142	.056
17	—.007	—.006	—.547	—.062	—.124	.135
18	—.391	—.376	—.072	—.641	.084	—.196
19	.743	—.157	—.015	.043	.039	—.406
20	—.028	—.178	—.096	.040	—.840	.242
21	.394	—.280	.051	—.461	.436	.001
27	.175	.070	.783	—.165	.005	.312
34	—.046	.671	.341	—.103	.061	.102
35	.117	.083	.013	—.728	—.021	—.080
37	.134	—.047	.073	—.562	.220	.235
39	.697	.004	.192	—.210	.309	—.057
44	—.905	—.081	.012	—.036	—.123	—.120
45	—.090	.073	.250	—.769	—.129	—.374
46	—.493	.098	—.028	.060	.012	.711
47	.081	.414	—.256	—.617	—.335	—.175
49	.504	.120	—.083	—.005	.424	.275
50	—.330	—.335	—.053	.105	—.651	—.366

[a] Variable numbers are defined in Table 2

Factor 2 appears to be a residual factor.

There is not sufficient information to define Factor 3.

Factor 4 is interpreted as a "consumption-elimination" factor. The
loadings here involve food and water consumption during the night (Vs.
45, 47), urination (Vs. 35, 37), and defecation (Vs. 18, 21). Since
body weight (V. 17) is not present in this factor, the factor is consumption-elimination, rather than size.

Factor 5 is called "field exploration." Open-field activity scores (Vs.
20, 50) as well as number of crossings in the novel stimuli box and the
social stimulus box (Vs. 5, 6) load highly on this variable. Defecation in

the open field (Vs. 21, 49) has loadings on this factor with the opposite sign.

It is not possible to define Factor 6.

When an oblique rotation was used, the same factors emerged and were fairly orthogonal to each other.

Discussion

The results of the factor analysis were intellectually very satisfying. The finding of a meaningful factor structure ". . . establishes the important general conclusion that stable individual differences can be created by experimental means independent of any contribution by genetic variance" (Whimbey & Denenberg, 1967a). The stability of these individual differences over time was clearly established since the last experimental treatment terminated at 42 days of age, at which time all animals were housed under common conditions, and experimental testing did not begin until 220 days of age.

The finding that the factor of emotional reactivity emerged from the data was an important empirical verification of this construct within the context of early experience research, and supported the basic assumption present in Denenberg's (1964) theoretical paper.

Another important contribution that these data make to theory concerned the nature of the constructs of exploration and emotionality. These were found to be two independent behavioral dimensions rather than opposite ends of a bipolar factor. This means that early experiences can independently affect emotional reactivity and exploratory behavior. Support for this conclusion has also been found under very different experimental procedures (DeNelsky & Denenberg, 1967a, 1967b; Denenberg & Grota, 1964).

Still another contribution of these data concerns the meaning of the activity and defecation scores in the open-field test. Defecation was found to have its major loadings on the factor of emotional reactivity while the activity variable loaded both on the exploration dimensions as well as on the emotional reactivity dimension. Furthermore, activity on the first day in the open field correlated positively with defecation scores and had a positive loading on the emotionality factor while activity scores from Day 2 onward correlated negatively with defecation scores and had a negative loading on the emotionality factor. These findings are discussed in detail elsewhere (Whimbey & Denenberg, 1967b; Denenberg, 1969b).

These results raise a very tantalizing and very important theoretical question. The factor structure obtained in this analysis was surprisingly similar to those obtained when heterogeneous groups of rats or mice were used in factor analysis studies (Anderson, 1938a, 1938b; Willingham, 1956). There are two possible explanations for this finding: (1) experimental manipulations during early life can bring about as large and complex a range of individual differences as can random genetic variation, or (2) the random and uncontrolled experiences that animals have as they grow and develop may be playing a much more important role in establishing individual differences than has previously been realized.

Q-Type Factor Analysis

In addition to the R-type analysis described above, a Q-type analysis was also carried out with respect to the independent variables. To do this analysis the 16 experimental groups in Table 1 were correlated across 20 of the tests listed in Table 2. Six factors were extracted and submitted to an orthogonal rotation. Since the experimental design contained only four independent variables, it was difficult to identify the six factors extracted. These data therefore will not be discussed and the reader is referred to the original articles (Whimbey & Denenberg, 1967a) for the statistical findings.

The Q-type analysis does offer certain methodological advantages, and I would like to note these briefly. Suppose that two groups (of the 16) load positively on the same factor or factors. What does this mean? Obviously their behavioral profiles on the test battery must have similar shapes in order for the two groups to load on the same factor. In other words, the correlation of these two groups across their profile of tests must be positive. As defined by this particular battery of tests, the experiences that these two groups have received may be considered to be functionally equivalent to some degree. We have called this approach "the psychophysics of experience." (This equivalence between two or more groups is only with respect to the test profile. Neither the correlation coefficients nor the factor loadings tell one anything concerning the elevation of the profiles.)

This approach of the psychophysics of experience can be used to investigate the question of "therapy" for reversing the effects of early experience and may also be used to investigate the critical period hypothesis. The reader is referred to the original article for a discussion and examples of these two concepts (Whimbey & Denenberg, 1967a).

PROGRAMS OF EXPERIENCE AND THEIR EFFECTS UPON LATER BEHAVIOR

The factor analysis results described earlier established that stable and relatively permanent complex individual differences, of the sort often assumed to be genetically determined, could be generated by the appropriate manipulation of experiences during early life. Three behavioral dimensions were isolated by the factor analysis: emotional reactivity, exploratory behavior, and consumption-elimination. Since the nature of the experimental design eliminated genetic factors as causal determinants of these behavioral dimensions, their existence was determined solely by the various programs of life experiences engendered via our experimental manipulations. To understand the causal determinants, analyses of variance were done on those tests that had high factor loadings on one or more of the three factors isolated in Table 3. Table 4 lists those tests that helped in defining the three behavioral dimensions and in which there was at least one significant analysis of variance main effect, exclu-

TABLE 4

Loadings on the Three Factors for Those Tests Which Yielded
Significant Analysis of Variance Results
Loadings Considered in Defining the Factors Are Boxed In
(From Denenberg and Whimbey, 1968)

DEPENDENT VARIABLE	EMOTIONAL REACTIVITY	EXPLORATORY BEHAVIOR	CONSUMPTION ELIMINATION
Emotionality rating	.697	.309	—.210
Boluses in learning unit	.743	.039	.043
Novelty box: time	—.529	—.188	.431
Open-field boluses	.394	.436	—.461
Novelty box: crossings	—.418	—.636	.057
Open-field activity	—.028	—.840	.040
Open-field activity: retest[a]	.054	—.805	.213
Open-field latency[a]	.041	—.847	.017
Social box: crossings	—.228	—.777	—.132
Food consumption: night	—.090	—.129	—.769
Water consumption: night	.081	—.335	—.617

[a] All factor loadings from Whimbey and Denenberg (1966) except these which were derived from data in Whimbey (1965).

sive of sex. The first five variables in Table 4 defined the emotional reactivity factor. Exploratory behavior was defined by the fifth through the ninth variables listed in that table. Consumption-elimination was described by the fourth, tenth, and eleventh variables.

A qualitative summary of the analysis of variance findings of the variables listed in Table 4 is given in Table 5. Certain generalities can be drawn from the statements in Table 5. The major experience bringing

TABLE 5

Qualitative Summary Relating the Analysis of Variance Findings
to the Three Factors in Table 4.
(From Denenberg and Whimbey, 1968)

Factor Variable	Significantly Modified by	Effect
Emotional Reactivity	Handling pups in infancy (5 of 5)[a]	
	One interaction	Reduces emotionality
Exploratory Behavior	Handling pups in infancy (3 of 5)	Increases exploratory behavior
	Handling mothers during their infancy (3 of 5)	Decreases exploratory behavior
	Seven interactions	
Consumption-Elimination	Handling pups in infancy (1 of 3)	Decreases defecation
	Handling mothers during their infancy (1 of 3)	Decreases food intake
	Postweaning housing in free environment (1 of 3)	Decreases water intake
	Two interactions	

[a] Numbers in parentheses indicate number of significant effects out of total number possible. For example, five tests defined the factor of emotional reactivity (Table 4); in all instances the Offspring Handling main effect was found to be significant.

about the changes in emotional reactivity was the handling that pups received in infancy. Those that were handled were less emotional than nonhandled animals. Only one interaction was found to be significant, thereby indicating that the effects of handling are invariant over the other experimental manipulations introduced into this study. Handling, therefore, is a very robust variable.

The pattern of findings is quite different when one examines those variables that affected exploratory behavior. Here also, handling pups in infancy is a significant variable leading to an increase in exploratory behavior. Pups born and reared by females who were themselves handled in infancy are less exploratory, however, an interesting reversal from expectation. Equally as important is the finding that seven interactions were significant for this dimension. We interpret this to mean that the dimension of exploratory behavior is complexly determined by the particular schedule of experiences that an animal has throughout his lifetime (including its mother's infantile experiences) and that no one single event is primarily a determining factor for this behavior. This is in sharp contrast to the emotional reactivity dimension, which seems to be more or less set and fixed by one major experience.

At this time there is insufficient information to draw any general conclusions concerning causal variables modifying the consumption-elimination factor except to indicate that the handling experiences that both the mothers and their pups received did act upon the behaviors defining this factor.

Patterns of Experience and Open-Field Activity

The factor analysis data showed that the variable of open-field activity was a measure of the dimension of exploratory behavior.[2] We had also done another experiment using the same four independent variables as used in the factor analysis study; open-field activity scores were obtained on those animals as well (Denenberg, Karas, Rosenberg, & Schell, 1968). That study was split with part of the animals first getting their open-field testing at 70 days while others first received open-field testing at 190 days. They were tested for 3 days in a row, which differs from the Whimbey and Denenberg factor analysis study in which animals were tested for four days in a row in the open field beginning at 220 days of life.

Even with these procedural differences, the studies are similar enough so that comparisons may be made among them with respect to open-field activity. This affords us the opportunity of determining which of the 16 programs of life history experiences gave us consistent results from one study to another. It also gives us a basal reference point against

2. Scores on the open-field activity variable were also found to be related to the emotional reactivity factor. The relationship changed on different days, however, so that open-field activity summed over four days did not load highly on emotional reactivity in the present study. The relationship between open-field activity and emotional reactivity is presented elsewhere (Whimbey & Denenberg, 1967b).

which one can compare other types of manipulation that are superimposed or interimposed upon these schedules.

The mean activity scores for the 16 groups in each of the three studies are presented in Table 6. (The fact that the absolute value of these scores changed from one experiment to another is not relevant here. The experiments differed with respect to the number of days of testing in the open field and the age of the animal, both of which affect absolute performance. The important consideration here is the relative difference among groups.) If one rank orders these groups within each experiment and then seeks consistency among experiments, it is possible to isolate 10 programs of experience that give roughly uniform results within each of the replications. These programs of experience are presented in Table 7 in rank order from that experience schedule resulting in least activity in the open field to that schedule resulting in the greatest activity. Although rank order is not perfect among the three studies, the inversions are of a relatively minor nature.

The importance of Table 7 is in demonstrating that the "pattern" of experiences is crucial in determining exploratory behavior. Consider the first, the fifth, and the tenth programs listed in Table 7. In each instance the animals were reared in free environments from birth until 42 days of age. Even though intuitively one feels that such enrichment should lead to greater exploratory behavior, it is apparent that the rearing habitat may act to maximize or to minimize exploratory behavior as a joint function of the handling experiences that the mother and her pups receive during their respective infancies. The same general finding is observed when one examines the fourth and the eighth experience schedules in Table 7: here animals were maintained in laboratory cages all their lives and the only difference in their experience was the handling that the mothers and the pups received. In this instance the rank order results parallel those observed when animals were raised in free environments all their lives. One should not take this to mean that the stimulation given the mothers and their young via handling is more important than the rearing environment in which the animals are maintained. For example, the difference between the eighth and the tenth programs in Table 7 concerns the nature of the habitat since the experiences that the mothers and pups received are identical. In that comparison the habitat would be naïvely thought of as the "cause" of the activity differences.

At this point all we can do is report these data in a descriptive fashion. We do not know why these particular programs of experience give

TABLE 6

Mean Open-Field Activity Scores for Each of Three Replications

(From Denenberg, 1969c)

Mother's Experience	Offspring's Experience	Preweaning Housing	Postweaning Housing	Denenberg et al. (1968), 70-day data	Denenberg et al. (1968), 190-day data	Denenberg & Whimbey (1968), 220-day data
NH	NH	MC	LC	79.2	54.9	40.3
NH	NH	MC	FE	48.8	59.8	111.3
NH	NH	FE	LC	80.4	56.1	102.3
NH	NH	FE	FE	63.8	91.7	23.0
NH	H	MC	LC	101.1	58.8	141.6
NH	H	MC	FE	56.4	25.2	29.0
NH	H	FE	LC	124.2	35.4	86.7
NH	H	FE	FE	182.0	82.1	253.7
H	NH	MC	LC	82.0	48.2	10.0
H	NH	MC	FE	85.5	23.2	57.0
H	NH	FE	LC	56.6	57.9	17.0
H	NH	FE	FE	45.0	48.0	8.0
H	H	MC	LC	119.4	58.9	155.3
H	H	MC	FE	145.0	49.0	39.3
H	H	FE	LC	31.8	19.2	120.3
H	H	FE	FE	81.2	57.3	34.7

NH = nonhandled in infancy, H = handled in infancy, MC = maternity cage, LC = laboratory cage, FE = free environment

TABLE 7

Mean Open-Field Activity Scores for Those Programs of Experience from Table 6
Which Gave Consistent Results for the Three Replications

Programs Listed in Rank Order
(From Denenberg, 1969c)

Mother's Experience	H	NH	H	H	H	NH	NH	NH	H	NH
Offspring's Experience	NH	H	NH	NH	H	NH	NH	H	H	H
Preweaning Housing	FE	MC	FE	MC	FE	MC	FE	MC	MC	FE
Postweaning Housing	FE	FE	LC	LC	FE	LC	LC	LC	LC	FE
Denenberg et al. (1968) 70-day data	45.0	56.4	56.6	82.0	81.2	79.2	80.4	101.1	119.4	182.0
Denenberg et al. (1968) 190-day data	48.0	25.2	57.9	48.2	57.3	54.9	56.1	58.8	58.9	82.1
Denenberg & Whimbey (1968) 220-day data	8.0	29.0	17.0	10.0	34.7	40.3	102.3	141.7	155.3	253.7

consistent results across experiments except to make the rather obvious statement that the differences appear to be some complex function of the four variables involved. Perhaps equally as important is the observation that six of the programs in Table 6 do not give consistent results across experiments.

The value of these findings, I believe, is that it demonstrates that we have been able to develop a procedure that will give us a reproducable phenomenon with respect to experiential determinants of an important behavioral dimension, namely, exploration. Hopefully, further research will enable us to understand the dynamics of the interactions that I have described in this report.

Effects of Stressors in Adulthood upon Patterns of Experience

The 10 schedules of experience listed in Table 7 were chosen because they gave generally consistent rank order results within each of the studies. Given such a stable reference point, one can now superimpose other sets of experiences upon this background to see how the criterion score of open-field activity is modified. In the Denenberg, Karas, Rosenberg, and Schell (1968) paper the animals that were first tested at 70 days in the open field (see Tables 6 and 7 for their data) were then given 50 avoidance-learning shuttlebox trials over a five-day interval and were then retested in the open field at 190 days of age. Other animals that had not received any test experience at 70 days underwent 60 hours of total food and water deprivation when they were 100 days old. They were also given the open-field test at 190 days. These two groups, which received different forms of stress experience in adult life (avoidance-learning testing or food and water deprivation), may be compared with a group of animals that received no stress experience in adulthood, namely, the 190-day group. The results of that experiment have been discussed in detail elsewhere (Denenberg et al., 1968) and the discussion here will be limited to the consequences of these stress experiences upon the pattern of scores reported in Table 7. Table 8 presents the same schedules of experience as Table 7 and also repeats the data for the 190-day group that received no prior experience. Below that group are listed the scores of the animals that received open-field testing from 70 to 72 days and avoidance learning testing from 73 to 78 days. And below that group are the open-field activity scores for those animals that underwent 60 hours of food deprivation starting at 100 days of age.

TABLE 8

Effects of Adult Stress Experience Upon Open-Field Activity for
10 Selected Programs of Life Experiences
All Testing at 190 Days
(Data from Denenberg et al., 1968)

Mother's Experience	H	NH	H	H	H	NH	NH	NH	H	NH
Offspring's Experience	NH	H	NH	NH	H	NH	NH	H	H	H
Preweaning Housing	FE	MC	FE	MC	FE	MC	FE	MC	MC	FE
Postweaning Housing	FE	FE	LC	LC	FE	LC	LC	LC	LC	FE
No prior adult experience	48.0	25.2	57.9	48.2	57.3	54.9	56.1	58.8	58.9	82.1
Open-field testing, 70–72 days and avoidance testing, 73–77 days	45.5	14.8	66.6	35.6	39.3	43.5	70.5	45.5	36.8	102.8
Food and water deprivation, 100–102.5 days	39.5	33.6	67.6	27.0	59.3	31.9	43.2	29.1	57.1	44.6

It is immediately apparent that the consistency of findings seen in Table 7 are not present in Table 8. A simple way of describing this is via the rank-order correlation. In Table 7 the rank-order correlation between the 190-day data and the 70-day data is .79 while the correlation between the 190-day data and the 220-day data is .78. This is in contrast to Table 8 where the correlation between the group receiving no adult experience and the animals receiving avoidance learning training is .51 while the correlation is .47 between those animals receiving food deprivation experience and those with no adult experience. Furthermore, the rank-order correlation between the food and water deprived group and those receiving avoidance learning training is only .34. We may therefore conclude that adult stress experiences as typified by avoidance training or food and water deprivation are sufficient to modify the rank-order brought about by the four variables programmed into the early life histories of our experimental subjects, but the two forms of stressors do not have equivalent effects upon the profiles of the groups.

Another example of this general finding is seen in a study by Denenberg, Rosenberg, Haltmeyer, and Whimbey (1969) who investigated the effects of crowding stress and food deprivation upon the open-field activity of rats. They worked with animals whose mothers were non-handled controls and who were born and reared in maternity cages and laboratory cages throughout their lives. The pups were either handled or nonhandled during their infancy. These conditions represent the sixth and eighth groups in Table 7 and the data of those two groups are reproduced in Table 9. In addition, the results of the Denenberg study (Denenberg et al., 1969) are seen in Table 9. The animals that were handled in infancy were found, at 90 days, to be more than twice as active in the open field than the nonhandled controls, findings consistent with the other data in that table. Furthermore, crowding immediately after weaning did not change this pattern of results nor did food deprivation when each of these variables was manipulated singly. For the group that received both crowding experience and food deprivation, however, there was a drastic reversal in the pattern of the means as seen in the last line of Table 9.

A final example of how adult experiences can act to modify the patterns of experience laid down by early programming is a study by Denenberg and Rosenberg (1969) in which the female offspring of handled and nonhandled mothers were studied. We have previously found (Denenberg & Whimbey, 1963, 1968) that offspring of non-

TABLE 9

Effects of Crowding and Food Deprivation Stress Upon Open-Field
Activity of Handled and Nonhandled Rats

Mother's Experience	NH	NH
Offspring's Experience	NH	H
Preweaning Housing	MC	MC
Postweaning Housing	LC	LC
Denenberg et al. (1968)	79.2	101.1
70-day data		
Denenberg et al. (1968)	54.9	58.8
190-day data		
Denenberg & Whimbey (1968)	40.3	141.7
220-day data		
Denenberg et al. (1969)		
90-day data	71.83	163.00
+ Crowding	82.67	123.83
+ Food Deprivation	55.33	103.50
+ Crowding and food	114.67	68.17
deprivation		

handled mothers were more active in the open field than offspring of
handled mothers. We repeated that finding with half of the females in
the Denenberg and Rosenberg (1969) study. The other half of those
females were given additional experience in adulthood, namely, that
of getting pregnant and bearing and rearing a litter. At the time of weaning these females were given the open-field test as well. We obtained
results exactly opposite to our prior findings: those females that had been
born and raised by handled mothers were now more active than those
born and raised by nonhandled mothers.

What do all these results mean? Two things are clearly apparent:
(1) any notion that the effects of early experiences are irreversible is
false, and (2) the data firmly reject any critical period hypothesis which
demands that certain experiences must occur at certain specified ages
or times in order for an organism to develop in a normal fashion (see
Denenberg, 1968, for an extensive discussion of the critical period hypothesis). Aside from these rather general statements I do not believe
there is sufficient data available as yet to make any very definitive
statements. I am satisfied that we have developed good methodological
techniques for manipulating programs of experiences, and I think that
we have shown clearly that one can obtain meaningful behavioral dimensions and reproducible results from one experiment to another. Also, as

one superimposes additional experiences upon an animal that has already been programmed, still further changes in the behavioral profile (as defined by our open-field activity measure) can be obtained.

Prenatal and Postnatal Maternal Effects

Before concluding I would like to describe our first experiment in this general research area and then report on a recent extension of that experiment. Our research with the rat had shown that our procedure of handling the animal in infancy had very wide and profound effects upon the behavior and physiology of the adult animal. It seemed reasonable to ask whether the handling experience the female rat had during her infancy would affect her offspring. Such effects could be brought about during the fetal period as a function of physiological changes induced in the mother by the handling she had received in infancy, or they could occur after birth as a result of physiological changes affecting the milk supply or behavioral changes affecting the pattern of mother-young interactions. We set up an experiment in which handled and nonhandled females either reared their own young from birth to weaning or else the young were cross-fostered both within and between handled and non-handled groups. We are concerned here only with the fostered groups because from that design it is possible to separate prenatal from post-natal contributions to behavior. Table 10 presents the experimental design and the findings for activity in the open field.

TABLE 10

Mean Open-Field Activity Scores of Rat Offspring as a Function of the Infantile Experiences of Their Natural Mother and Their Rearing Mother
(From Denenberg and Whimbey, 1963)

Infantile Experience of Prenatal Mother:	Not Handled		Handled	
Infantile Experience of Postnatal Mother:	Not Handled	Handled	Not Handled	Handled
Mean Activity:	114.9	188.4	139.6	121.5

A significant interaction between prenatal and postnatal experiences was found, and it is clear from examining Table 10 that those animals whose natural mothers were nonhandled and who were reared by handled mothers were significantly more active in the open field than the other three groups (Denenberg & Whimbey, 1963). We conclude from these data that the handling experience that these mothers had received in their infancy had profound changes upon their physiology and biochemistry to such an extent that the in utero interactions between mother and fetus differed from that occurring in nonhandled control animals, and this difference, in combination with the consequences of being reared by a handled mother from birth onward, was sufficient to change the behavior of these animals.

Grandmothers Are Important Too

Having shown that experiences that females have in infancy will affect both the behavior and physiology of their offspring, one begins to wonder how far these effects can be pushed. The grandmother is the logical next step in this search and we have found significant effects here as well (Denenberg & Rosenberg, 1967). The experimental design and results are given in Table 11.

TABLE 11

Mean Open-Field Activity Scores as a Function of Grandmother's
Infantile Experience, and Mother's Rearing Habitats
(From Denenberg & Rosenberg, 1967)

GRANDMOTHER'S EXPERIENCE	MOTHER'S PREWEANING HOUSING	MOTHER'S POSTWEANING HOUSING	MEAN ACTIVITY
NH	MC	LC	32.0
NH	MC	FE	44.3
NH	FE	LC	22.4
NH	FE	FE	27.1
H	MC	LC	29.7
H	MC	FE	35.5
H	FE	LC	49.8
H	FE	FE	28.8

We started out with female rats that were handled or nonhandled in infancy. They were maintained in maternity cages or laboratory cages until adulthood and were then mated. When pregnant these animals were placed either into maternity cages or free-environment boxes and the animals that were born in these units became the mothers of our experimental subjects. At the time of weaning, the female pups were placed into laboratory cages or free-environment boxes where they remained until they were 50 days old. At that time all animals were placed into laboratory cages where they remained until mature when they were mated. All animals gave birth to their offspring in standard maternity cages. At weaning these pups (who were the grandchildren of the original handled and nonhandled mothers of the study) were given one day of testing in the open field. Their activity scores are presented in Table 11. The following interactions were found to be significant: Grandmother Handling x Mother Preweaning Housing, Grandmother Handling x Mother Postweaning Housing, and Preweaning Housing x Postweaning Housing. Some understanding of the nature of these interactions can be gleaned by looking at the first and the fifth groups of Table 11. Both of these groups are animals raised under standard maternity and laboratory conditions, and it can be seen that there is very little difference in the mean activity of the grandpups. The occurrence of an enriched experience either before or after weaning in the early life of the mothers of these pups was a necessary condition for the effects of the grandmothers' handling experience to express itself.

We may conclude that the experiences during one's infancy may be visited upon one's descendents two generations away if one's children live in the appropriate ecology during early life.

Again, let me emphasize that I believe these studies show that we have the appropriate methodology to manipulate complex sets of variables that extend not only throughout an animal's lifetime but also across several generations. We have, however, very little idea of the nature of the mechanisms involved. The search for mechanism is the next step in our course of programming life experiences.

REFERENCES

Anderson, E. E. The interrelationship of drives in the male albino rat: II. Intercorrelations between 47 measures of drive and learning. *Comparative Psychology Monographs*, 1938, **14**, No. 8. (a)

Anderson, E. E. The interrelationship of drives in the male albino rat: III. Interrelations among measures of emotional, sexual, and exploratory behavior. *Journal of Genetic Psychology*, 1938, **53**, 335–352 (b).

DeNelsky, G. Y., & Denenberg, V. H. Infantile stimulation and adult exploratory behavior: Effects of handling upon tactual variation seeking. *Journal of Comparative and Physiological Psychology*, 1967, **63**, 309–312. (a)

DeNelsky, G. Y., & Denenberg, V. H. Infantile stimulation and adult exploratory behaviour in the rat: Effects of handling upon visual variation-seeking. *Animal Behavior,* 1967, **15,** 568–573. (b)

Denenberg, V. H. Critical periods, stimulus input, and emotional reactivity: A theory of infantile stimulation. *Psychological Review,* 1964, **71,** 335–351.

Denenberg, V. H. Stimulation in infancy, emotional reactivity, and exploratory behavior. In D. C. Glass (Ed.) *Neurophysiology and emotion.* New York: Rockefeller University Press and Russell Sage Foundation, 1967, Pp. 161–190.

Denenberg, V. H. A consideration of the usefulness of the critical period hypothesis as applied to the stimulation of rodents in infancy. In G. Newton & S. Levine (Eds.) *Early experience and behavior.* Springfield, Ill.: Thomas, 1968. Pp. 142–167.

Denenberg, V. H. The effects of early experience. In E. S. E. Hafez (Ed.) *The behaviour of domestic animals* (2nd ed.). London: Bailliere, Tindall & Cox, 1969, in press. (a)

Denenberg, V. H. Open-field behavior in the rat: What does it mean? *Annals of the New York Academy of Science,* 1969, in press. (b)

Denenberg, V. H. Experimental programming of life histories in the rat. In J. A. Ambrose, (Ed.) *The functions of stimulation in early postnatal development.* London: Academic Press, 1969, in press. (c)

Denenberg, V. H., Brumaghim, J. T., Haltmeyer, G. C., & Zarrow, M. X. Increased adrenocortical activity in the neonatal rat following handling. *Endocrinology,* 1967, **81,** 1047–1052.

Denenberg, V. H., & Grota, L. J. Social-seeking and novelty-seeking behavior as a function of differential rearing histories. *Journal of Abnormal and Social Psychology,* 1964, **69,** 453–456.

Denenberg, V. H., Karas, G. G., Rosenberg, K. M., & Schell, S. F. Programming life histories: An experimental design and initial results. *Developmental Psychobiology,* 1968, **1,** 3–9.

Denenberg, V. H., & Morton, J. R. C. Effects of environmental complexity and social groupings upon modification of emotional behavior. *Journal of Comparative and Physiological Psychology,* 1962, **55,** 242–246.

Denenberg, V. H., & Morton, J. R. C. Infantile stimulation, prepubertal sexual-social interaction, and emotionality. *Animal Behavior,* 1964, **12,** 11–13.

Denenberg, V. H., Ottinger, D. R., & Stephens, M. W. Effects of maternal factors upon growth and behavior of the rat. *Child Development,* 1962, **33,** 65–71.

Denenberg, V. H., & Rosenberg, K. M. Nongenetic transmission of information. *Nature,* 1967, **216,** 549–550.

Denenberg, V. H., & Rosenberg, K. M. Programming life histories: Effects of maternal and environmental variables upon open-field behavior. *Developmental Psychobiology,* 1968, **1,** 93–96.

Denenberg, V. H., Rosenberg, K. M., Haltmeyer, G. C., & Whimbey, A. E.

Programming life histories: Effects of stress in ontogeny upon emotional reactivity. *Merrill Palmer Quarterly,* 1969, in press.

Denenberg, V. H., & Smith, S. A. Effects of infantile stimulation and age upon behavior. *Journal of Comparative and Physiological Psychology,* 1963, **56,** 307–312.

Denenberg, V. H., & Whimbey, A. E. Behavior of adult rats is modified by the experiences their mothers had as infants. *Science,* 1963, **142,** 1192–1193.

Denenberg, V. H., & Whimbey, A. E. Experimental programming of life histories: Toward an experimental science of individual differences. *Developmental Psychobiology,* 1968, **1,** 55–59.

Hunt, H. F., & Otis, L. S. Early "experience" and its effects on later behavioral processes in rats: I. Initial experiments. *Transactions of the New York Academy of Science,* 1963, **25,** 858–870.

Levine, S. A further study of infantile handling and adult avoidance learning. *Journal of Personality,* 1956, **25,** 70–80.

Levine, S. Infantile experience and consummatory behavior in adulthood. *Journal of Comparative and Physiological Psychology,* 1957, **50,** 609–612.

Levine, S. Noxious stimulation in infant and adult rats and consummatory behavior. *Journal of Comparative and Physiological Psychology,* 1958, **51,** 230–233.

Morton, J. R. C. The interactive effects of preweaning and postweaning environments upon adult behavior. Unpublished Ph.D. dissertation, Purdue University, 1962.

Ottinger, D. R., Denenberg, V. H., & Stephens, M. W. Maternal emotionality, multiple mothering, and emotionality in maturity. *Journal of Comparative and Physiological Psychology,* 1963, **56,** 313–317.

Spence, J. T., & Maher, B. A. Handling and noxious stimulation of the albino rat: I. Effects on subsequent emotionality. *Journal of Comparative and Physiological Psychology,* 1962, **55,** 247–251.

Whimbey, A. E. The factor structure underlying the experimentally created individual differences studied in "early experience" research. Ph.D. dissertation, Purdue University, 1965.

Whimbey, A. E., & Denenberg, V. H. Programming life histories: Creating individual differences by the experimental control of early experiences. *Multivariate Behavior Research,* 1966, **1,** 279–286.

Whimbey, A. E., & Denenberg, V. H. Experimental programming of life histories: The factor structure underlying experimentally created individual differences. *Behaviour,* 1967, **29,** 296–314. (a).

Whimbey, A. E., & Denenberg, V. H. Two independent behavioral dimensions in open-field performance. *Journal of Comparative and Physiological Psychology,* 1967, **63,** 500–504. (b).

Willingham, W. W. The organization of emotional behavior in mice. *Journal of Comparative and Physiological Psychology,* 1956, **49,** 345–348.

Comments on Denenberg's "Experimental Programming of Life Histories and the Creation of Individual Differences: A Review."

CHARLES DARBY
University of Georgia

I WOULD LIKE to preface my remarks about Dr. Denenberg's report by noting the vantage point from which I work. I am interested in animal behavior in an evolutionary context. I am neither a statistician nor a psychometrician, hence I will not attempt statistical evaluation of Dr. Denenberg's work. Since I have known Dr. Denenberg personally for some years and served on the Purdue faculty with him for four of these, my comments derive as much from having watched him work as from anything that appears in his report.

In the main, his report is conservative. It reflects nearly a decade's work by Dr. Denenberg and his colleagues and students. The data are copius and the conclusions drawn appear to be consistent with them. Extrapolations are few and carefully identified as such. Homage has been paid to the complex causality of behavior and the need for further research.

I would first like to summarize the report as I read it. To begin with, while it is not stated, I am judging that all the data reported were obtained from either Harvard-Wistar or Purdue-Wistar rats, which the author refers to as a "large group of homogeneous animals." Two variables were manipulated—handling and environmental complexity— handling prior to weaning of the test subjects and their mothers, and environmental complexity to 42 days of age for the test subjects. Some 180 days later, the subjects were tested in a variety of ways designed to assess emotional reactivity, socialization, and exploration. These data were analyzed a la the psychometrician and the following major conclusions drawn or reaffirmed: (1) Stabile individual differences can be created by experimental means independent of any contribution by genetic variance. (2) Emotional reactivity is reduced as a monotonic function of amount of stimulus input in infancy. (3) Early experience can independently affect emotional reactivity and exploratory behavior. (a) The major contribution to emotional reactivity was handling. Handling is a very robust variable. (b) Emotional reactivity seems to be set and fixed by one major experience. (c) Exploratory behavior is complexly determined. The pattern of experience for exploratory behavior is crucial.

In addition to the data from which the above conclusions were drawn, data were reported that reflected the effects of various stressors upon patterns of adult behavior derived from infantile experiences. In essence, it was found that different stressors had different effects and that two stressors presented together had an effect while either of the stressors presented alone did not. Adult experiences could and did modify the effect of early experiences.

From these data it was concluded that "Two things are clearly apparent: (1) any notion that the effects of early experiences are irreversible is false, and (2) the data firmly reject any critical period hypothesis which demands that certain experiences must occur at certain specified ages or times in order for an organism to develop in a normal fashion."

Finally, although far from least importantly, Denenberg presents data indicating "that the experience during one's infancy may be visited upon one's descendents two generations away. . . . Grandmothers are important too."

As I said at the outset, Denenberg's report is conservative. Denenberg and his co-workers have carefully and methodically pursued their studies of the effects of infantile (or early) experiences upon adult behaviors in white (Wistar) rats. Their conclusions are well within keeping with the data. Their methodological innovations provide a valuable guide for additional work.

To evaluate the findings, the individual differences created in these studies are, by virtue of the design employed and the subjects used, "independent of any contribution by genetic variance." Their findings with respect to the emotionality dimension are consistent with those from studies of other laboratory rodents.

The degree of generality of these conclusions, while in all likelihood great, must await work with other strains and species. One is reminded of the extended debate between the Tolmanians and the Hullians about the nature of learning, a debate arising from data that Jones and Fennell (1965) suggest might just as easily have derived from the "genetic" makeup of the rat subjects as from any mode of learning.

The definitions of and distinctions between emotionality and exploratory behavior and their experiential antecedents suggest productive next steps in the study of these variables both in terms of the experimental techniques by which the distinctions are drawn and the theoretical import of the distinctions.

With respect to the conclusions regarding the existence of critical periods and the irreversibility of the effects of early experience, I agree with Denenberg, certainly to the extent of agreeing that both concepts are in need of refinement. This conclusion is, however, unique to neither me nor Denenberg (Sluckin, 1965). More importantly, I believe that the required refinements are to be found in Denenberg's own data. Whether the term applied to the period be "critical," "sensitive," or "optimal," what is implied is some sort of differential plasticity associated with the age and/or experience of the animal. Clearly, it is difficult, at least with respect to "psychological" variables, to demonstrate a sharply defined period within which a behavior can be induced and outside of which it cannot. It is a matter of the ease or economy of the induction of the behavior rather than an either-or affair. This posture seems to be entirely consistent with Denenberg's referring to handling during infancy as a "very robust variable," i.e., a variable having a greater impact on adult emotionality than any of the other variables manipulated. It is stated that ". . . the emotional reactivity dimension . . . seems to be more or less set and fixed by one major experience."

While the existence of critical periods re "psychological" inputs may be in doubt, the same would not appear to be the case with respect to "physiological" variables. Mullins and Levine (1968) state that: "It has now been well established that a single injection of either testosterone propionate (TP) or estradiol benzoate (EB) given to female rats during infancy profoundly alters the subsequent reproductive physiology and behavior of the animals. The effects depend on the dose and hormones used and the exact time during early life that the injection is given."

The other issue was the irreversibility of behavior. The term "irreversible" has about it the same categoric nature that weakens the term "critical" when applied to a phenomenon such as behavior. If we would substitute another term or phrase, as has been done for "critical," I think we can preserve an important notion, namely that the integrity of any given behavior is differentially susceptible to the impacts of subsequent experiences, some have an effect, others do not. Whimbey and Denenberg (1967) discussed the effects of "therapy," i.e., the effects of postweaning experiences in reversing the effect of early experience. Citing Denenberg and Morton (1962), they noted that a given experience was "therapeutic for one combination of preweaning experiences but not for another combination." In other words, the effects of one set of experiences could be reversed but the effects of another could not. It would seem to me to be important to understand both what induces susceptibility to therapy (reversal) and what induces resistance to therapy. Why are the effects of some experiences reversible and others not? Also, what therapies are effective?

In this context, in discussing the effects of stressors on adult behavior, it was reported that different behaviors yield to different stressors and that the summing of stressors can have an effect not obtained from the application of a single stressor. "Therapy" involves not only "what kind" but "how much."

As was the case with "critical period" we find physiological data less equivocal than the "psychological" data. Dubos, Schaedler, and Costello (1968) studied the effects of maternal diet on the growth rates of specific-pathogen-free (SPF) mice. They found that "In SPF mice nursed by their own mothers, the diet of the latter during gestation and lactation, or during lactation alone, conditioned the weight of the young at weaning time and throughout their whole life span." In manipulating maternal diets, they found some diets whose effects on the weight of offspring were irreversible and others that were not.

The Dubos et al. study and the earlier reference to "physiological" effects, beg the question of where the line between "physiological" and "psychological" is to be drawn. What, for example, would be the case in studying the effects of the injection of substances designed to mimic the internal chemical or hormonal changes associated with ECS and studying the effects of ECS by itself?

The space given the "grandmother" data hardly does justice to their import. It is not enough that we must worry about schizophrenogenic mothers; we now have grandmother on our back. The procedures designed to elucidate the mechanisms by which such effects are transmitted are apt to be as exciting as the data themselves.

Denenberg concludes that we have, however, very little idea of the nature of the mechanisms involved. The search for mechanisms is the next step in our program of programming life experiences."

I have no notion what route their search will take but I would like to refer briefly to an example of the kind of theorizing or speculation that might prove quite valuable in guiding the search. Bronson (1965) has proposed a model designed to relate the ontogeny of behavior to the maturation of the central nervous system. He develops a hierarchical model of CNS functioning to which he relates a hierachy of learning processes in the context of which he discusses critical period phenomena. One of the critical periods defined by Bronson is the "period affecting the later 'emotionality' of the animal with the sensitive period occurring directly after birth and with the amount of general (unpatterned) stimulation as the significant variable. . . ." He attributes the characteristics of this period to the primacy, during the period immediately following birth, of the system composed of the brain stem motor nuclei and reticular system, a system responsive to the mode or intensity of stimulation but not to the patterning within modes. This latter capacity must await the maturation of a higher, Level 2, network comprising the thalamus, hypothalamus, and limbic system.

Without further elaboration, I believe that such modeling is a potentially valuable guide on which to base the study of the nature of the relationships that represent the next stage or stages in the program that has been undertaken by Denenberg.

I see little or no conflict between Denenberg's views and mine. He is to be commended for the tenaciousness with which he has pursued the program he has undertaken and the most inventive way in which he has analyzed, presented, and interpreted the data.

REFERENCES

Bronson, G. The hierarchical organization of the central nervous system: Implications for learning processes and critical periods in early development. *Behavioral Science*, 1965, **10**, 7–25.

Denenberg, V. H. & Morton, J. R. C. Effects of environmental complexity and social groupings upon modification of emotional behavior. *Journal of Comparative and Physiological Psychology,* 1962, **55,** 1096–1098.

Dubos, R., Schaedler, M. D., & Costello, R. Lasting biological effects of early environmental influences. *The Journal of Experimental Medicine,* 1968, **127,** 783–799.

Jones, M. B. & Fennell, R. S. Runway performance in two strains of rats. *Florida Academy of Sciences Quarterly Journal,* 1965, **28,** 289–296.

Mullins, R. F., Jr. & Levine, S. Hormonal determinants during infancy of adult sexual behavior in the male rat. *Physiology and Behavior,* 1968, **3,** 339–343.

Sluckin, W. *Imprinting and early learning.* Chicago: Aldine, 1965.

Whimbey, A. E. & Denenberg, V. H. Experimental programming of life histories: The factor structure underlying experimentally created individual differences. *Behavior,* 1967, **29,** 296–314.

The Distancing Hypothesis:
A Causal Hypothesis for the Acquisition
of Representational Thought[1]

IRVING SIGEL
The Merrill-Palmer Institute

INTRODUCTION

THE CENTRAL PROBLEM in this paper is the identification of transformation rules and the conditions relevant to defining the transition
from a sensorimotor to a representational mode of thinking. This transition occurs during the later part of the second year of life when the infant
shifts his thinking from nonrepresentational to representational thought
(Piaget, 1962). The child becomes capable of reconstructing reality into
images, symbols, and other kinds of signals that are manifestations and
re-presentations of the social and physical reality.

The aims of this paper, then, are to discuss the context within which
to view the issues relevant to the transition from a sensorimotor and/or
three-dimensional view of the world to representational reconstruction of
reality; to present data from a variety of sources that aided in the defini-

1. Portions of this paper were presented at the American Psychological Association Annual Meeting, September, 1968. I wish to thank Miss Joan Bliss, University of Geneva, Dr. Marjorie Franklin, Bank Street College, and Dr. William
Overton, State University of New York at Buffalo, for their careful reading of
the manuscript and their advice in helping reduce conceptual confusion and
obscurantism in this paper. Failure to achieve this is my responsibility. Dr.
Franklin helped stimulate the discussion on language.

Some of the research reported in this paper was funded by Office of Economic
Opportunity Contracts #542, #1410, and #4118.

tion and subsequent conceptualization of the issue; and to present a hypothesis by which to test the theoretical formulation.

STATEMENT OF THE ISSUES

Initially, it is assumed that intrinsic to man's adaptation to his ostensive environment is the capability of employing symbol or sign systems by which to reconstruct that environment mentally. Man has the potentiality to devise systems by which to condense and to combine the array of diverse physical and social stimuli he encounters in the course of his existence. In this way man creates order. This ability is expressed in the construction of category systems by which environmental instances in some representational form are organized and to which particular behaviors are associated.

Categories provide the means of organization of knowledge and of behavioral response repertoires that the individual uses to effect adaptation to the environment. Categorizations, however, evolve as a function of an array of sociocultural learnings.

The argument in this paper is based on the fundamental premise that the ostensive world is one of three dimensions where objects (animate and inanimate) are palpable and are perceived in their solidity and depth either as instigators of actions or as recipients of actions. It is this ostensive environment in all its complexity and diversity that becomes transformed (reconstructed) into mental or symbolic representations, e.g., images, pictures, etc. These representations furnish data that are stored and/or utilized in the course of building classifications. This brings us to the central theme, namely the process and conditions involved in transforming the three-dimensional environment into its representations. For example, how does the individual learn to recognize or realize that the three-dimensional world can be represented in two dimensions?

Representations are acquired initially and perhaps all through life in the course of interactions with three-dimensional reality. These representations form bases for action in lieu of the presence of the realities, e.g., responses to pictures that are derivatives or generalizations or equivalents to that three-dimensional reality. The child responds to his mother and to a picture of his mother with full knowledge the latter is a representation of his mother. The recognition that the picture is a representation, i.e., stands for or in place of the mother, is a significant developmental accomplishment. We do not yet know how the child comes to this awareness. How does he learn that objects and events can be represented with fewer dimensions?

I wish to study the "hows" and "wherefores" of the development of representational thought in a psycho-cultural context. Every culture devises some type of representation and fosters it. This representation is no doubt functional in its particular context. Specifically, for now, the aim is to focus on the cognitive processes involved in the acquisition of representation in Western society, since such intellectual achievement is a necessity for adaptation to a complex industrial and technological environment. For maximal effectiveness in such a society, the acquisition of symbol-signal using skills is necessary. These are in essence representations of functioning conceptual systems. These conceptual systems comprise the logic and/or the rationale of the categorization system as well as the content of the category. First, the individual learns how to group and what to group. These involve a variety of cognitive processes (Inhelder & Piaget, 1964). In a complex technological culture many categories exist and many items exist within each category. For example, let us look at the category of transportation. If one compares the variety of paraphernalia utilized to transport objects or people in our country in contrast to an underdeveloped one, a wide array of items are found, ranging from simple carts and handdrawn vehicles to those that are flying around or toward the moon—indeed a large content for this category. We have in addition many categories. The categories and their contents are represented by a complex symbol-signal system. For example, the category transportation can be depicted in pictures, words, sounds. Each of the modalities have the same concrete referent. Further, elaborate systems exist for graphic and auditory symbol representational depiction of the environment. These representations serve to instigate behavior, provide the means of retaining information, and enable communication in the absence of the ostensive world. The significance of representational thought speaks then to the need to understand how we learn to adapt and to function at this level. In essence, the question is, as posed at the beginning of this discussion, what are the conditions, the requirements, and the rules by which the individual develops the competence to deal with the world representationally.

A survey of the research literature reveals an amazing lack of theoretical and empirical information explaining the acquisition of representational skills and competence. Such theorists as Piaget (1962), Werner and Kaplan (1963), and Bruner (1966) are among the major figures who have addressed themselves to this question.

Let me start from the proposition that representation is generic to man, but the kinds of representations and what is represented are acquired as functions of particular experience. Man reconstructs the environment in symbolic forms. He does re-present it in various modes, e.g., memories, images, pictures, etc. We can thus dispense with the issue of the capability for representation and direct attention to the how and what man represents, how and what representations function in terms of influence on retaining and utilizing knowledge. These become some of the relevant domains for research in cognitive psychology.

How man thinks, what man remembers, what man perceives, and what man does with the knowledge that he acquires, are derivatives of, and dependent on, man's basic capability to represent the world in mentalistic terms. We tend to take for granted that ability to deal with the world representationally is a given. In so much of our psychological research we take for granted that the subjects are all intrinsically functional on a representational level. For example, just think that most of the experimental stimuli employed in research in perception, in learning, in memory, and in thinking are re-presented material. Pictures, sounds, various kinds of visual stimuli of a graphic order, all of these are the stimuli to which the organism is asked to react. Our measures of intelligence tests for the most part contain graphic symbols. In effect, studies employ representations or graphisms, and therefore it is to that reality our subjects respond. Is it not ironic that much of what we know about cognition is based on response systems to representations—yet we know little about this first step. It is as though we start in the midst of the behavioral stream. Undergirding all these response capabilities is the accepted idea that the individual has this response capability to representational stimuli. I shall present an array of data from a variety of sources that clearly shatters the assumption that man "naturally" responds to representation, that children automatically have the response repertoire by which to evoke or employ representational thought, even with stimuli as presumably simple as photographs of familiar objects. In this paper I will show that children's ability to deal with representations of their environment is indeed a function of the life experiences and will vary accordingly.

SOME DATA ON REPRESENTATIONAL COMPETENCE

Turning to the data upon which these assertions are based, I will begin with a study I reported in 1953. At that time I reported that lower-middle-class boys with average mental ability, when asked to classify familiar items, employed similar categories for classification irrespective of the level of symbolization of the stimuli (Sigel, 1953). Free-sorting tasks were used, employing three-dimensional toys, black and white pictures of these toys, and words (names of the items). The items used were in the following categories: vehicles, furniture, animals, and people. The results of this study indicated that the boys, irrespective of age and level of representation, tended to use similar kinds of classification. I concluded, therefore, that the level of representation, i.e., the object, picture, or word, was not a necessary relevant dimension for these boys, aged 7, 9, and 11. The relevant dimension was the meaning of the object, i.e., the definition the child gave the object. It was this meaning that transcended the physical or graphic representation of the object. To put it another way, the meaning attributed to an object was not changed by alteration of the mode of representing that object (Sigel, 1954). The intrinsic meaning of the object is conserved, i.e., is maintained, in the face of transformations, and the child is not confused by variations in the mode of representation. The ability of the child to respond in such a consistent manner is designated as *representational competence,* i.e., the ability to deal competently and equivalently with representational material.

Many years later, when I resumed work in cognitive styles, I decided to pretest some black and white photographs of familiar items in order to create a sorting task. The only school available contained the age groups we needed, namely children 5 and 6, but was predominantly a lower-class black school. We assumed that in view of our previous research that the social class might not really be a very relevant variable, so I blithely proceeded to present my black and white pictures in the usual format to these children. I discovered that they had difficulty classifying the pictures. They tended to associate them by chaining, frequently thematically rather than on the basis of class membership or common properties. Items selected tended to bear little or no functional relationship to previous or subsequent choices. A typical performance would be one in which the child selects a picture of an object and then chooses a second one as related to the first, but a third choice is not selected as related to the first. Why did these children tend to have such difficulty in simple, free classification tasks? Two questions come to mind. Do these children lack the skills needed for classifying objects, or do these children have difficulty because the stimuli are pictures? I was inclined to reject this second presentation since the children were able to label the items in each picture correctly, and the results of the earlier study had shown no differences in classification. I had no reason to believe that the mode of representation was at issue. I was inclined to think that these children lacked the capability to abstract, in this sense, to search for commonalities and to build classes. An astute kindergarten teacher quickly disabused me of this notion when she said that the correct labeling of the picture does not necessarily indicate the child understands that picture. The children could not group pictures, she explained, because they lack the awareness that the picture was in fact a representation. It disturbed me to receive such a sophisticated answer from the teacher. Why could we not have thought of this? Such wisdom is frequently overlooked by researchers as significant contributions. Believing that the teacher was dead wrong, but with a nagging doubt regarding my own judgment, I decided it was necessary to repeat the format of the earlier classification studies with lower-class children using three-dimensional objects and their two-dimensional counterparts. In essence, I replicated the 1953 study. For a more stringent comparison between "real" and representational objects I decided to use three-dimensional life-sized objects instead of toys, since toys are actually representations.

Two sorting tasks were created containing three-dimensional life-sized objects, each familiar to lower- and middle-class children, e.g., cup, pencil, pipe, etc., and two-dimensional colored photographs of these objects blown up to approximate as close as possible the size and color of the objects. (See Figure 1.) A number of studies were done comparing grouping performance with the two- and three-dimensional tasks. The results revealed that the teacher was indeed right, the mode of representation of the items posed a problem for the children. The grouping of three-dimensional objects by lower-class children did not differ significantly from that of the middle-class children. The grouping of pictures between the two socioeconomic groups revealed significant differences, where nongrouping responses were significantly greater for lower-class children, showing that lower-class children have greater difficulty making groups with pictures than with the objects. Lower-class children find it easier to group three-dimensional objects in contrast to pictures. This is not true for the middle-class child (Sigel, Anderson, Shapiro, 1966; Sigel & McBane, 1967). These findings were indeed surprising in the face of the fact that the lower-class black children did have language, a system of signs, and could use this language to label the objects. Is it not said that language when considered a sign is in fact representational? If this is so, how is it that these children lack representational competence?

Four other sets of data helped solidify the interpretation that lower-

FIG 1.

class black children had difficulty in coping with representation in the form of the nonpresent or the inferential or re-presentation of reality.

The first is based on performance results with a group of preschool underprivileged children on the Motor Encoding Test of the Illinois Test of Psycholinguistics. It will be recalled that in this task the child is presented with a black and white picture of an object and asked to show in gestures only what is done with the object. This task is one of the most difficult ones for these underprivileged children between 3 and 5 years of age (Sigel & Perry, 1968). If the child, however, is given a three-dimensional version of the same object depicted in the picture, he has less difficulty in acting out, again in gestures, the function of the object. When given the actual object, he has no problems at all, even if unable to label it.[2]

What makes the grouping task more difficult with pictures than three-dimensional objects? Could it be that in the three-dimensional condition the child has a wide array of cues, and perhaps more than that, he has the gestalt of the object in its spatial locale, its palpability, which are more congruent with his own active experience with objects. Three-dimensional objects have a greater action-evocation potential than pictures. Should not pictures as representations, however, have the same action evocation if the picture is an acknowledged representation of the object? If the child is truly capable of representational thought, the difference between the object and the picture conditions should be nonsignificant.

A second piece of evidence comes from doll play situations with lower-class black children. The child was presented with a male adult doll, a female adult doll, and a like-sexed doll. The child was asked to tell a story using the three dolls. No other props were used. With prompting and prodding, the children provided a series of action-packed, reality-based stories, i.e., the presentation of plausible situations that appear to be reenactments of life rather than the types of condensation of symbolism so frequently associated with the more middle-class children. Very few importations were used. Instead the actions attributed to the individuals were just descriptions of the acts they used between the objects. The lower-class child rarely used words to refer to inner feelings or inner thoughts. The stories were primarily statements of immediate

2. These observations occurred in the course of a Preschool Evaluation Study under the sponsorship of the Detroit Board of Education, and the supervision of Mr. Burt Pryor and Dr. Donald Friedheim, Western Reserve University.

actions and interactions with little reference to the past or to the future.

A third source of evidence emerges from observation of play behavior of lower-class black children where the play of these children appears to be motoric, action based, with minimal use of imagery or pretending or role playing.

This type of play behavior is not unique to black lower-class children. Smilansky reports similar results with Israeli children who originally came from underprivileged Middle-Eastern backgrounds. She found that most of the cuturally disadvantaged children "do not play dramatic play at all, and those who do, play only in the especially equipped corners. Even the few plays that are organized and maintained for some time differ considerably from the average play of advantaged children" (Smilansky, 1968, p. 150).

We can now ask the question, is this difficulty in dealing with representations solely a function of disadvantage in a particular culture. The answer to this question will be forthcoming in a series of studies undertaken to assess the differential role of three- and two-dimensional stimuli in some types of cognitive functioning, especially memory. Second, review of some anthropological research clearly shows that cultural differences in representational thought exist.

I would like to present some evidence to show that (a) the picture-object response discrepancy is not unique to lower-class children, and (b) that this discrepancy is not unique to this particular group of lower-class children. Let us first turn to a discussion of the significance of dimensionality in memory, thereby addressing ourselves to the degree to which dimensionality as a relevant variable transcends the social status of the individual. Dr. Joseph P. Jackson is involved in a series of studies at the Merrill-Palmer Institute investigating the role of dimensionality in short- and long-term memory. He has discovered in working with seven-year-old middle-class privileged children that these children tend to be better in the recall of three-dimensional objects as compared with two-dimensional objects. Presenting a series of pairs of items, either three-dimensional or two-dimensional, he discovered that the children tended to remember the three-dimensional pairs more frequently than the two-dimensional pairs 24 hours later. This suggests then that there is a superior recall with three-dimensional stimuli. The explanation of this phenomenon is still moot but it does suggest that the materials are not dealt with equivalently (Jackson & Abramsky, in preparation; Sigel & Jackson, in preparation).

A number of studies done in the field of learning and/or retention with adults have found that objects tend to be more frequently recalled or more easily learned than words.

The differential responses to pictorial representation, and perhaps representation in general, vary among cultural groups—which brings us to our fourth set of evidence, namely cultural differences in response to representations.

Hudson presents an interesting review of the major studies that have been done in South African countries. Examining the role of pictorial representation, these studies show convincingly that Bantu speaking tribesmen had difficulty in perception of pictures as representations of three-dimensional reality. Hudson provides a vivid description of the phenomenon.

> Two of the pictures, all of which were unambiguous half-tone graphic representations, produced unexpected perceptual responses in twenty protocols. One scene, representing the homecoming of a migrant industrial worker, contained the figures of an elderly couple seated in the traditional way on the ground. Behind, was a thatched round hut with the figure of a worker, clad in overalls, arms akimbo, superimposed upon it. Seven protocols referred to a winged being, a devil, an angel, the temptation of Eve in Paradise. By accident, the artist, in superimposing on the hut the foreground figure of the worker, had placed the ragged thatched roof of the hut in such a position that an observer, who perceived pictures two-dimensionally, could see the thatch as feathers or wings sprouting from the figure's back just above his shoulders. The posture with arms akimbo aided this perception" (Hudson, 1967, p. 93).

Difficulties exist not only in this type of pictorial perception but also in depth perception where relative object size overlapping perspective posed problems for the subjects. Just as one illustration, Hudson reports that when he presented photographs to the subjects more than one quarter of the Bantu pupils perceived them in two dimensions, although the pictures could be perceived in three-dimensional ways. By the end of primary school, white pupils were competent in viewing these pictures in three-dimensional perspective, but the same conclusion did not hold up for black pupils. In other words, "the depth perception performance of the more highly educated black samples was not significantly better than that of the white school children of the upper class in the primary school" (Hudson, 1967, p. 95). The implications of this difference in perspective are considerable. "Lack of understanding of the convention of perspective reduced comprehension and rendered the material of little value for teaching, and pictorial symbols capable of a literal or extended meaning tended to be interpreted literally by people of limited education" (Hudson, 1967, p. 105).

Cultural differences are not only found in regard to response to representational material in the form of pictures but also perceptual non-representational stimuli. Segall, Campbell, and Herskovitz (1966) report cultural differences in response to perceptual illusion, e.g., Muller-Lyer. They claim that cultural groups vary in their susceptibility to illusions because of variable experiences in particular ecological settings.

All these studies raise the following questions:

Why the discrepancy in object-picture classifications?

Why the discrepancy in performance on the motor-encoding task between the three-dimensional condition and the picture condition?

Why are the story telling and play so heavily weighted in the direction of motoric-action level with minimal imaginative role playing or as-if play?

Why the cultural variations in perspective with two-dimensional stimuli?

REPRESENTATION: A THEORETICAL AND DEFINITIONAL ANALYSIS

In effect, the basic question is what accounts for the deficit in representational competence?

Posing the question this way stimulated first a search of the literature for conceptualization of representation. Piaget (1962), Werner and Kaplan (1963), and Bruner (1966) are the major writers who have defined the phenomena.

For Piaget, "Representation is characterized by the fact that it goes beyond the present, extending the field of adaptation both in space and time. In other words it evokes what lies outside the immediate perceptual and active field" (Piaget, 1962, p. 273). He goes on to say, "Accordingly representation can be used in two different senses. In its broader sense representation is identical with thought, i.e., with all intelligence which is based on a system of concepts, on mental schemas, and not merely a perception of actions. In its narrower sense, representation is restricted to the mental or memory image, i.e., the symbolic evocation of absent realities" (Piaget, 1962, p. 67).

Bruner has recently offered some conceptions of representation. He has proposed three stages of representation: enactive, ikonic, and symbolic. The enactive refers to motoric behaviors, the ikonic to imagery, and the symbolic to language (Bruner, Olver, & Greenfield, 1966).

For Bruner, "There are two senses in which representation can be understood: in terms of the *medium* employed and in terms of its objective. With respect to the first, we can talk of three ways in which somebody 'knows' something; through doing it, through a picture or image of it, and through some such symbolic means as language. . . . understanding between the three can be achieved by viewing each as if it were external" (Bruner et al., 1966, p. 6). The objective of representation for Bruner seems to be a guide to action.

Werner and Kaplan deal with the concept of representation in the context of symbols, where the term symbol is used in two senses: "in one, it is employed when we wish to emphasize a fusion or indissolubility of form and meaning; in the other, it serves to designate a pattern or configuration in some medium (sounds, lines, body movements, etc.) Insofar as the pattern is taken to refer to some content" (Werner & Kaplan, 1963, p. 15). Symbols are "entities which subserve a novel and unique function, the function of *representation*. The function of representation is a constitutive mark of a symbol; it distinguishes anything qua symbol from anything qua *sign, signal,* or *thing*" (Werner & Kaplan, 1963, pp. 13–14).

Representation, then, involves a reconstructing of the world of objects, thereby leading to actions guided by such representations.

On the basis of the theoretical discussion of representation presented earlier, let it be made clear that re-presenting is the process of reconstruction of reality that can be external or internal, while representation is the product or outcome of re-presenting. Objects can be represented by pictures or symbols, photographs, drawings, art forms, etc. Internal representation takes the form of imagery or schematization of reality in various degrees. Representations contain minimum fractional elements of the reality depicted. Representations, therefore, can vary in content. An image of a ball is a representation, as in a picture; a map also is a representation but is *schematic*—a representation of physical environment. The mental image of a ball or of one's spouse's face is internal, the picture of the ball is external. Representational competence refers to the individual's capability to respond appropriately to external representations, to behave in terms of internal referents, to reconstruct nonpresent reality.

Representations are distal from the sensorial world. They are re-presented, not in their palpable form. Representations are not intrinsic to the object or the event, they are a depiction of reality—in time, space, and content. The child has to learn that the representation is a mode of depicting instances of the physical and social world—modes that are distinct from their referent.

For some, language is also to be considered as a form of representation (Bruner et al., 1966). This is not my view. My definition of representation does not include language since language is considered as a system of signs that can function to evoke representations. (Language may also evoke nonrepresentational behaviors, e.g., expressiveness and action). Language also depicts representations such as verbal descriptions of objects or events. The event can thereby be reconstructed (imagery) or anticipated. Language serves as the vehicle by which the speaker signals to the hearer with the outcome evocation or representations. The possible exception here is onomatopoeic language or some poetic rhythms that generically overlap in some formal way with the referent (object or event).

Before concluding the discussion of the concept of representation, it should be made clear that the effort here is to speak in operational and objective terms, i.e., using the physical palpable reality as the point of departure. To be sure, a picture is a re-presentation of that object. Using the physical and/or external environment as the touchstone against which determination of representation is to be made, can be disputed. Representations can be viewed as having their origin in the eyes of the beholder. Very young children respond to photographs by trying to remove the object from its ground—Church refers to this as picture realism (Church, 1961). For some children physical objects can also be viewed as representations.

THE DISTANCING HYPOTHESIS

Acquisition of representational competence is hypothesized as a function of life experiences that create temporal and/or spatial and/or psychological distance between self and object. "Distancing" is proposed as the concept to denote behaviors or events that separate the child cognitively from the immediate behavioral environment.

The behaviors or events in question are those that require the child to attend to or react in terms of the nonpresent (future or past) or the nonpalpable (abstract language). Distancing stimuli can emanate from persons or events, e.g., the mother and child discussing an anticipated birthday party or the child searching his toy chest for a particular favorite toy.

The child adapts to these situations by developing and utilizing representation. It is in this sense that representation is viewed as adaptive.

Distance is expressed in the stimuli themselves. For example, a cutout picture of a chair is closer to the chair, or less distal, than is the word chair, simply because the latter contains no overlap of any kind with the actual reality of the chair. A photograph, for example, may be more distal than the cutout, since the cutout contains some notion of dimension or depth in its physical form, whereas the picture (photograph) only represents depth through particular visual cues. The term distal will be used to refer to the distance within the domain of the stimuli. Distancing refers to acts or events that may or may not employ distal stimuli to create the separation or differentiation between self and the physical environment.

In sum, then, two terms are introduced, distal, referring to the nature of the stimulus, and distancing, referring to those classes of behaviors and events that separate the person from the environment.

The distal construct is consonant with Piaget's, Bruner's, and Werner and Kaplan's conceptualization of representational behavior. In each case there is the implicit or explicit statement that the representations of reality are separated from reality by physical or psychological distance. Be it the image, the picture, the symbol, or the sign, each one is distant in varying degrees from its referent.

The set of events that are hypothesized as significant determinants for the development of representation are distancing ones—where distal stimuli may or may not be employed. As we shall see, the point of view of this paper stresses the role of distancing experiences for the child, with the distal media furnishing some of the communication modalities. For example, a parent may describe in very vivid language an anticipated event, e.g., a trip; or a parent in preparing a child for a hospitalization experience might employ a picture book depicting hospital events to be experienced. These types of communications probably stimulate the child to image, to anticipate, in effect, to represent the nonpresent events.

The distance may be temporal, as between a past event and a present recall; spatial, as with a picture or image and the pictured or the imaged; in its modality, the name and the object; or in degree of detail, a sketch of an object and the object itself.

Distancing is a way to characterize differentiation of the subjective from the objective, the self from others, ideas from actions. Representational competence is hypothesized as the resultant of experiences creating such distance.

The foregoing statements are based on the assumption that man has the generic capability to respond to distancing by creating representations of reality; the actualization of representational competence depends on the distancing experiences as part of the broader culture as well as the particular life history.

The technological urbanized culture in the United States is a society that employs distancing and requires the construction of representations to a large extent. The time emphasis, the transmission of knowledge through pictorial representation, and/or graphic signs all involve representational competence.

Since these are demands of the broader cultural system as expressed in our educational system and in our middle-class environment, the difficulty found among these lower-class children becomes poignant, particularly for the Negro children. That the latter in particular have difficulty at the kindergarten level speaks to the possibility of continuing difficulty in school, particularly when it comes to those cognitive requirements prerequisite for academic performance.

Study of the conditions creating distance and the subsequent acquisition of representation is proposed as a research strategy in order to contribute to the remediation for those children having difficulty and also hopefully to extend our knowledge of a crucial cognitive acquisition —that of representational competence.

A search of the empirical research literature, aside from the classification studies mentioned earlier, is of little comfort. To be sure, some studies have demonstrated that levels of representation do in fact effect the quality of responses. Pictures elicit different responses than words in class inclusion problems (Wohlwill, 1968). Use of three-dimensional materials influence solution to conservation problems differently than verbal presentations (Sigel, Saltz, & Roskind, 1967). But on the whole, other than the work of Bruner, Piaget, and Werner and Kaplan, few detailed empirical studies are available investigating origins and functioning of representation among children.[3]

We are, therefore, left with a major research task, the discovery of the conditions that define the necessary and sufficient conditions for the es-

3. There are a number of memory and learning studies among adults comparing the relative difficulty in retention of pictures versus words, or objects versus words.

tablishment of representational competence. In the remainder of this paper I shall offer some specific hypotheses by which to test the distancing hypothesis.

Initially it was believed that differences in intellectual performance between lower- and middle-class children could be attributed to differences in distancing experiences in the first two years of life. Life for the lower-class child is very different from that of the middle-class child. Apparently the differences during the first two years of life are not sufficient to differentiate cognitive performance between lower- and middle-class Negro children (Golden & Birns, 1968).

Such distancing experiences may provide the basic ingredients upon which representational competence can be built. These may well be the necessary conditions, but subsequent interactions with the social world may provide the sufficient conditions. No socioeconomic status differences in tasks involving the displacement of objects, search for missing objects, and Cattell IQ are found. These findings suggest that at the preverbal age (before 2) children from varying environments do have the ability to recall the existence of an object and to anticipate its location (Golden & Birns, 1968). Performance on such tasks indicates that rudimentary representation of the object and its place in space is present.

On the basis of these data one is left with the conclusion that differences between lower- and middle-class children in intellectual functioning found at later ages may well have their roots in the transitionary period, the last stage of the sensorimotor intelligence and the beginning of preoperational thought, approximately that period between 2 and 4 years. It may well be that it is during this period of life that the adult assumes a more significant psycho-social role in increasing distance between self and object and hence contributes to the development of representational competence.

During this transitional period, language and extended social contacts occur. My contention is that during this period significant experiences begin to occur, experiences necessary for acquisition of representational thought. It is at this time in the life of the child that lower-class parents behave differently from middle-class parents in how they interpose in terms of time, space, and language to create distance between the child and his environment.

The experiences necessary for the acquisition of representational thought are presumed to occur through the parents' provision of: (1) a relatively orderly, structured, and sequential environment; (2) a linguistic environment that contains a high frequency of words denotative of distance between referent (object) and level of language (concrete-descriptive versus abstract-inferential); (3) models indicating the relevance and pragmatic value of distancing.

Each of these conditions is hypothesized as contributing significantly to the development of representational competence because each facilitates the establishing of "distance"—spatially and temporally between objects and their referents. The rationale for each is as follows:

(1) The child must have an environment that is relatively orderly, structured, and sequential. The break in time-flow, the delineation of events that are nevertheless reiterated in coherent patterns, thereby structuring the world, are necessary. Consequently, predictability is possible not only because of the orderliness of the environment, but also because of the child's capacity for memory. These memories are particularly articulated when they serve gratification of needs. The result is the creation of a series of expectations, and expectations are really the anticipation of happenings. This anticipation is perforce represented at the preverbal level, perhaps by imagery (Decarie, 1965). In fact, there is a feedback cycle that occurs over time—programmed as follows—an event (present), memory for it (past), anticipation for reiteration (future). With the advent of language and stimulation to recall, evoked images are labeled and organized under particular rubrics. Language facilitates organization, because particular signs can encompass a wide array of instances. The degree of stability and predictability of the environment would be related to a high level representational performance.

(2) The content of the linguistic environment must contain a high frequency of words referring to time, space, distance, and reference to past, present, and future to create psychological distance between reality and its reconstruction. This is not to say just the use of language is enough, rather it is the quality of the language. As was indicated, the lower-class children in our study did utilize language, and yet they were poor performers. The hypothesis thus refers to the types of concepts that are used by the adults in the language. Lower-class children experience significantly greater concrete-motoric references and less abstract language than middle-class children (Hess & Shipman, 1964). Reality is thereby not reconstructed, and hence distancing is not so great among lower-class children. Language becomes the tool for, or the vehicle by which, objects and events can be distanced.

The grammatical structure of the language is also important. The way tenses are used expresses time concepts also. For example, it has been reported that in the language of lower-class Negroes, time is represented grammatically in the continuous present—"I does this"—which may refer to the past, present, or future. Clear-cut delineation of the three time dimensions is apparently not made. If this is true then some explanation is possible for the difficulty found among lower-class children. Since time is also reflected in sequencing of events, sequencing becomes another variable that contributes to the quality of the children's performances. The corollary hypothesis derived from such reasoning can be stated as follows: Representational competence is negatively influenced by the lack of time perspective concepts, those delineating distance in time past and future.

(3) The language and the orderliness of the environment can not account for all of the variance. There still must be opportunity for recall and reconstruction of the past, and planning for the future. By recalling events and stimulating discussion of what has happened, adults can give a child the opportunity to imitate them and participate with them in reconstructing the past. Such experiences are hypothesized as generating imagery for the experienced past event, thereby providing the groundwork for anticipatory responses. Correct anticipatory responses reveal to the child the orderliness and predictability of the world around him.

It can be argued that these three requirements place the burden of explanation on the quality and quantity of social interaction and offer very little in the way of psychological mechanisms that can be explanatory, but it must be kept in mind that the psychological mechanisms can not be viewed in isolation of the context that stimulates them. The research on sensory deprivation highlights the significant role of particular levels and quality of response as a function of such deprivation.

I have presented in a schematic and exploratory way some ideas and hypotheses regarding the development of representational competence. Refinement of the theoretical base is still necessary, delineating levels of representations, clarifying the conception of language, and spelling out in more operational terms the distancing hypothesis. Nevertheless, I believe the distancing hypothesis has a compelling logic that helps bring together much of the relevant theoretical literature and the few empirical studies. It helps to explain some of the data obtained with lower-class black children. The need, however, is to undertake experiments with very young black children at a preoperational level to test out these ideas. Time in this discussion provided only the opportunity to identify the problem and delineate some of the variables. The challenge is to construct significant tests of these hypotheses.

REFERENCES

Bruner, J. S., Olver, Rose R., & Greenfield, Patricia M. (Eds.). *Studies in cognitive growth.* New York: Wiley, 1966.

Church, J. *Language and the discovery of reality; a developmental psychology of cognition.* New York: Random House, 1961.

Decarie, Therese G. *Intelligence and affectivity in early childhood: An experimental study of Jean Piaget's object concept and object relations.* Trans. by Elisabeth P. Brandt & L. W. Brandt. New York: International University Press, 1965.

Golden, M., & Birns, Beverly. Social class and cognitive development in infancy. *Merrill-Palmer Quarterly,* 1968, **14,** 139–149.

Gollin, E. S. Factors affecting the visual recognition of incomplete objects: A comparative investigation of children and adults. *Perceptual and Motor Skills,* 1962, **15,** 583–590.

Hammond, K. R. (Ed.). *The psychology of Egon Brunswik.* New York: Holt, Rinehart & Winston, 1966.

Hess, R. D., & Shipman, Virginia C. Early experiences and the socialization of cognitive modes in children. *Child Development,* 1965, **36,** 869–886.

Hudson, W. The study of the problem of pictorial perception among unacculturated groups. *International Journal of Psychology,* 1967, **2,** 89–102.

Inhelder, Barbel, & Piaget, J. *The early growth of logic in the child: Classification and seriation.* New York: Harper & Row, 1964.

Jackson, J. P., & Abramsky, M. The effects of dimensionality in time: A comparison of the low- and middle-class child's recognition recall. (Article in preparation, 1969).

Piaget, J. *Play, dreams, and imitation in childhood.* Trans. by C. Gattegno & F. M. Hodgson. New York: Norton, 1962.

Segall, M. H., Campbell, D. T., & Herskovitz, M. J. *Influence of culture on visual perception.* Indianapolis, Indiana: Bobbs-Merrill, 1966.

Sigel, I. E. Developmental trends in the abstraction ability of children. *Child Development,* 1953, **24,** no. 2, 131–144.

Sigel, I. E. The dominance of meaning. *Journal of Genetic Psychology,* 1954, **85,** 201–208.

Sigel, I. E., Anderson, L. M., & Shapiro, H. Categorization behavior of lower- and middle-class Negro preschool children: Differences in dealing with representation of familiar objects. *Journal of Negro Education,* 1966, **35,** 218–229.

Sigel, I. E., & McBane, Bonnie. Cognitive competence and level of symbolization among five-year-old children. In J. Hellmuth (Ed.), *The disadvantaged child,* Vol. 1. Seattle, Washington: Special Child Publications, 1967, pp. 435–453.

Sigel, I. E., & Jackson, J. P. The efficacy of two- vs. three-dimensionality in children's recall of familiar objects. (Article in preparation, 1969).

Sigel, I. E., & Olmsted, Patricia P. Modification of classificatory competence and level of representation among lower-class Negro kindergarten children.

Final Report, Head Start 1966–67. In H. Passow (Ed.), *Education in depressed groups*, Vol. 2. New York: Columbia University, Teachers College Press, in press.

Sigel, I. E., & Perry, Cereta. Psycholinguistic diversity among "culturally deprived" children. *American Journal of Orthopsychiatry*, 1968, **38**, 122–126.

Sigel, I. E., Saltz, E., & Roskind, W. Variables determining concept conservation in children. *Journal of Experimental Psychology*, 1966, **4**, 471–475.

Smilansky, S. *The effects of socio-dramatic play on disadvantaged pre-school children*. New York: Wiley, 1968.

Werner, H., & Kaplan, B. *Symbol Formation*. New York: Wiley, 1963.

Wohlwill, J. Responses to class-inclusion questions for verbally and pictorially presented items. *Child Development*, 1968, **39**, 449–466.

Comments on Sigel's "The Distancing Hypothesis: A Causal Hypothesis for the Acquisition of Representational Thought."

C. D. SMOCK
University of Georgia

DR. SIGEL is to be congratulated for his courage, as well as his creative proposal for a direct attack on one set of determinants of representational competence. Despite the paucity of prior empirical data, he has managed to propose a number of antecedents of representational competence that provide a starting point for studying the mechanisms underlying representation. The distancing hypothesis is stated with such clarity that many derived empirical relations are obvious. Specifically, he hypothesizes that the acquisition of representational competence is "a function of life experiences that create temporal, and/or spatial, and/or psychological distance between self and object." These critical life experiences are presumed to be the following: (1) a relatively orderly and structured sequential environment; (2) a linguistic environment containing a high proportion of words denoting distance between referent or object and many abstract-differential terms (as contrasted to concrete descriptive); and (3) social models who indicate the relevant events and pragmatic value of the re-presenting process (anticipation and recalling).

The lack of much specifically relevant evidence on which to base a critical empirical evaluation of the hypothesis (a point on which Dr.

Sigel and I agree) forces me to concentrate more on the epistemological and theoretical problems associated with his proposal.

Decrease in "stimulus" control of behavior with increasing levels of ontogenetic development is an ancient, respected, and vague principle. Few theories of behavior have been able to give it sustained theoretical and empirical meaning. Modern developmental psychology has at least confronted behavior theories with an epistemological, theoretical, and methodological context that illuminates the complexity of the problem and yet holds some hope for the ultimate solution. The recognition of the critical importance of understanding the genesis of representational processes is, of course, one thing; the solution quite another.

Cursory examination of the many proposals for analysis of representational processes (e.g., Piaget, Werner, Bruner, Berlyne, and the Mediational theory) suggests the assumptive world of psychologists has changed dramatically during the past decade. Detailed analysis of these theories indicate otherwise; the change is not as drastic as some of the orienting propositions might lead one to believe. The study of early experience does not make a developmental psychology, nor does recognition of the principle of organism-environment interaction rid us of empiricism. The operational clarity of Dr. Sigel's proposal should not obscure its inherent complexities. The theoretical superstructure, with its methodological imperatives, is a sly intruder at several points in his analysis of representational competence and its antecedents.

Throughout the presentation, Dr. Sigel's commitment to a "real" environment is emphasized. Such an assumption appears necessary to avoid sterility and inactivity; but it is difficult to study "knowledge acquisition" processes without some consideration of alternative assumptions regarding the nature and role of the external world. It is of concern here, not because Dr. Sigel is unaware of the problem, but because of the inconsistencies that arise in the context of studying the role of "distancing" in the acquisition of representational processes. For example, a major purpose is to account for the "reconstruction of the world of ostensive objects and events"; or alternatively "the transformation of the ostensive world into representation"; and/or "the transformation rules governing representation beyond the present." The "reconstruction of the world of ostensive objects and events" appears to be a delimited problem that, with appropriate verbal gyrations, might just avoid most of these complexities; but the "transformational rules governing representation beyond the present" does not. That is, concern for the transformational rules governing representation beyond the present must involve, first of all, some consideration of the processes by which such events are initially represented and stored in memory.

Many psychologists appear to be moving toward the Piagetian position that emphasizes the relativity and constant development of our collective notions of reality and the increasingly complex system of interpretations of the environment. For example, physical reality can be considered a consequence of intellectual operations (e.g., conservation of length and distance) that make it possible for us to achieve intersubjective knowledge, i.e., the "objective external situation." The "ostensive" world of physical descriptions, then, is useful and necessary in the behavioral sciences in order to control input from outside the subject. It enables one to eliminate irrelevant influences and to single out psychological change and difference for study. One should not, however, reify our own constructions of the situation, or fail to remember that we are presenting the subject the product of our own cognitive processes.

Dr. Sigel, therefore, has a problem in maintaining consistency. On one hand, he insists on dealing with external, objective reality, and on the other hand, he commits himself to a cybernetic model and the discovery of transformation rules for retreiving (re-presenting) transformed information. Transformation of information requires some mechanism, but we are not given any indication of what such a mechanism might be, nor is it clear whether representational and re-representational processes involve the same or different transformational mechanisms.

Piagetian theory implies that the assimilatory schema, even enactive schema, have spatio-temporal "distal reference" and, therefore, simple recording of events does not occur without some element of inference or interpretation of feedback. In addition, modification of assimilatory cycles occurs not only as a function of disturbances induced by outside stimulation, but may well result from internal conflict. If we view these feedback effects as involving accommodatory activity, consisting in mutual adjustment of schema to each other, further delineation of the proposed antecedents of the "distancing" might be achieved. For example, it is hard to disagree with the proposal that degree of order structure and sequentiality of environmental events are important; but at the same time, it would seem that we should consider also: (1) the match between the current cognitive states and the degree of order; (2) the extent to which the sequentiality is imposed by the subject rather than environmental events; and (3) provision for optimal stimulus and cognitive-transformational activities. It is quite possible that one of the most important roles of language is to provide for cognitive conflict (conceptual mismatch) and transformational activities through evocation of conflicting "images." Dr. Sigel and I agree that it is doubtful that the mere labeling of past, present, and future events per se would be sufficient to account for the role of language in achieving subject-object differentiation and representational competence.

As participant processses in the emergence of higher level cognitive acquisitions, Dr. Sigel places considerable emphasis on the structure of the environment, and relatively little emphasis on the activity of the child.

Dr. Sigel emphasizes the current societial conditions that require representational processes for adaptation on the likelihood that representation is a generic capacity of homo sapiens. Certainly one of the critical emergent qualities of human evolution that insured survival has been the capacity to anticipate critical events (arrival of enemies, floods, etc.). Anticipation depends on the capacity to re-present (recall) prior experiences and the spatio-temporal patternings of selected environmental events. The emergence of the capacity to "re-present" depends critically on the differentiation of time and space as well as mechanisms for representing past events within a time-space frame of reference. The fact that children under three with differing cultural backgrounds do not respond differentially to objects and pictorial representations of external objects and events lends plausibility to Dr. Sigel's analysis.

One important implication of the above should be noted. Genetic capacities of a high developmental order may be detoured or suppressed if appropriate environmental pressures are not present during "optimum" periods of cognitive growth. It should be possible to identify the common "pool" of early or "pre-structures" necessary for development of symbolic representational processes and to determine whether the conditions Dr. Sigel cites are, in fact, critical to arresting hereditary programs of development or, perhaps, modify only the surface forms (phenotypical) of representation.